# contents

# foreword

Liz Klose

From prairie grasslands to meadows, woodlands, roadsides and even lawns, nature dresses the landscape in grasses. This family of plants has long been a staple food and provided shelter for humans and wildlife. More recently, grass has become the primary groundcover in home landscapes. This book, however, goes beyond the boundaries of grass as a green expanse of turf. Gardeners, more than ever before, are turning to ornamental grasses in their landscapes, using them in perennial beds and as sculptural elements and specimens.

This book demystifies grass terminology and reveals the plethora of colours in the ornamental grass palate. You will learn that ornamental grasses are superb companions to bulbs, conifers, shrubs and trees. The perennial companion section highlights just a few perfect partners. By knowing how to design with and care for ornamental grasses you will also discover innovative ideas for incorporating them in the landscape. The "Grasses at a Glance"

section is an especially useful summary.

Whether they are used in bold dramatic sweeps, as groundcovers and screens, or as focal points and container plants, grasses are tremendously versatile in any garden design. Their extended season of interest — from the moment they emerge in the spring to when they punctuate the blanket of snow in winter — adds to their importance as a design element.

Grasses have a linear quality that helps structure the garden. This can take various forms, from graceful fountain-like cascades and tufted mounds to towering open vase shapes and stiff upright spikes. Some grasses evolve through several different textures and forms, resulting in an ever-changing dimension in the garden throughout the growing season.

Grasses are relatively low maintenance; once established they are quite drought tolerant, with some selections performing very well in moist conditions. Most of the grasses detailed here are clump-forming grasses that are well behaved

# grass scapes

## gardening with ornamental grasses

Martin Quinn and Catherine Macleod

whitecap

Gardens are made by vision, hard physical work, tremendous humility and perpetual learning. This is also true of making books. In the creation of *Grass Scapes* I owe a lot to ornamental grass pioneers like Karl Foerster, Wolfgang Oehme and Kurt Bluemel. I am also grateful to Franz Peters, a fellow grower at Humber Nurseries in Toronto and friend Carolin Brooks, now of Owen Sound, who shared my earliest enthusiasm for ornamental grasses. I learned from authors, landscape architects, designers and educators like Liz Klose and Michael Pascoe, people whose work with ornamental grasses helped transform that early enthusiasm into a passion.

Very personal thanks, however, go to my first teachers, my parents Joyce and Harold Quinn, and to friends in local horticultural societies and Master Gardener groups.

I am grateful to those kind spirits whose interest and encouragement supported me as this book took shape — Lori Bale, Sheila Burr, Guiliana Colalillo, Jim Dalton, Liz Klose, Betty Lamont, Jennifer MacKay, Robby Macleod, Tyler Macleod, Doris Milne, Don Milne, John Melo, Jan Moyser, Vincenzo Pietropaolo and Julie Young. A special thanks goes to visual artist Wendy Hogenbirk for her skill in bringing grasses to life in watercolour. I also want to thank editor Elaine Jones for helping shape our book with patience and knowledge. She is a wizard. The courtly spirit of Robert McCullough and the diplomacy of Robin Rivers have made the creative journey both nurturing and nourishing.

Finally, I am grateful to my co-author and spouse, Catherine Macleod, who helped me find a way to make my grass scapes accessible and who opened that gate with love, faith and trust.

Martin Quinn, Kincardine, Ontario
January 2003

A true colourist can create harmony with 20 different reds. The reddest of red perennial grasses is *Imperata cylindrica* var. *koenigii* 'Red Baron' (Japanese blood grass). In this rock planting, 'Red Baron' illuminates *Eriophorum angustifolium* (cotton grass) and *Pennisetum alopecuroides* (fountain grass) growing nearby.

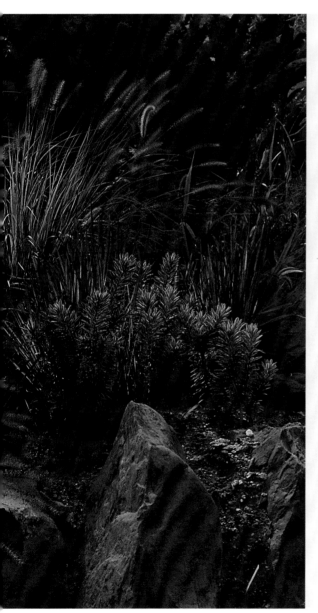

**Imperata cylindrica** var. **koenigii** 'Red Baron' (Japanese blood grass), **Eriophorum angustifolium** (cotton grass) and **Pennisetum alopecuroides** (fountain grass).

in the garden. Some spread slowly by rhizomes and others are more vigorous. The vigorous selections are best suited for ground covers or slope establishment. Essentially there is an ornamental grass for every habitat — naturalized or in a formal garden, in full sun or shade.

Far from being a monochromatic green, grass foliage comes in various hues, tints, and intensities of colour that change with the seasons. The inflorescences also have their own colour, ranging from purple to taupe, gold and eventually wheat.

Rustling and whispering, they lure us into our gardens. The flexible foliage bends and dances in the slightest breeze. Delicate seed heads catch the light. Morning sunlight illuminating dew or frost on the foliage is enchanting, as is the reflection of ornamental grasses nestled along the edge of a pond.

In *Grass Scapes*, Martin and Catherine have captured this magic.

# introduction

My mother was working in a flower shop in Guildford, England, during the Second World War when she met my father, a young soldier raised on a Canadian farm. Joyce Martin married Harold Quinn and moved with him to Kincardine, Ontario, where they set up a florist shop and nursery. Their small business in a small town flourished. As children, my sisters and I all helped out. We shared the joy of other families as they prepared for weddings or celebrated births; we also quietly shared their sorrows, delivering flowers of encouragement to hospital nursing stations and flowers of respect to funeral chapels.

My four sisters, Helen, Judy, Susan and Nancy, and I worked in our family greenhouses as far back as I can remember. We planted trees, designed gardens and laid sod. We seeded, divided and propagated. In travels all over the province with our father, we met and chatted with almost everyone who worked in the horticultural industry. My favourite task, however, was working in the enchanting gardens of gentle "ladies," who served me lemonade after the weeding, transplanting, grass cutting or trimming was done. When I finished high school I studied horticulture at Algonquin College in Ottawa and have worked in the industry ever since.

My interest in ornamental grasses began during a horticultural trip to England, Holland and Germany in 1985. At that time I became aware of the pioneering work of German horticulturist and perennial hybridizer Karl Foerster.

In Europe I saw ornamental grasses growing in climatic conditions very similar to those I knew in Canada and the northern U.S. I decided to test the common wisdom of the day and find out if they were hardy enough for Canada.

At the time I knew of no one growing ornamental grasses in Canada and had little information to help me select appropriate varieties (later I learned that Franz Peters at Humber Nurseries in Brampton was also interested in ornamental grasses). I began by importing and working with 85 grasses. This was before the electronic revolution that has made speedy online research possible, so it took me some time to discover that the same ornamental grass bug that had bitten Franz and I had also bitten three people in the U.S.

Kurt Bluemel, the acknowledged driving force behind the Ornamental Grass Movement in North America, had been working with grasses since the 1960s, when, as a student, he encountered their widespread use in Germany and Switzerland. When he moved to the U.S. his designs attracted attention in the Baltimore area, where he settled and opened a nursery.

Ornamental grasses were pushed further into the North American spotlight when landscape architect Wolfgang Oehme — a former Foerster student and Maryland neighbour of Bluemel — teamed up with Dutch-trained Jim Van Sweden. Oehme and Van Sweden used predominantly ornamental grasses in

### What is an ornamental grass?

The term "ornamental grass" is used very loosely. "True" grasses are members of the Poaceae family, which includes woody-stemmed bamboos. The other grass-like families are sedges (Cyperaceae), rushes (Juncaceae), restios (Restionaceae) and cattails (Typhaceae). Often sedges, rushes, restios and cattails are lumped in with true grasses when discussing ornamental grasses.

There are also a number of grass-like plants. For example, mondo grass (*Ophiopogon planiscapus*) looks like a grass and its common name makes it sound like a grass, but it is actually a dramatic lookalike that is not a grass at all.

Perennial grasses live and grow for decades. Annual grasses emerge from seed, grow, flower and die in one season. Some plants can be perennial in one climate and annual in another. In our gardens and this book, we focus on hardy ornamental grasses and sedges.

Although bamboo is actually one of the largest and oldest members of the Poaceae family, for now we use these manificent perennials primarily as companions to the other grasses we grow. Evergreen bamboos bring animation and an exotic look to the garden scene and are quickly earning a place in North American gardens.

# introduction

the redesign of the Federal Reserve Building in Washington, D.C. in 1977, sparking a horticultural revolution in the U.S.

In 1991 I met Michael Pascoe, Chief Horticulturist at the Cuddy Garden in Strathroy, Ontario, and he introduced me to Liz Klose of the School of Horticulture at Niagara Parks Botanical Gardens in Niagara Falls. She was undertaking a dramatic expansion of the grass gardens there. Liz called me about potential selections and I was happy to supply her with some new acquisitions.

In our own hardiness testing, in Strathroy first and now in our Kincardine greenhouses, we discovered that a number of varieties for Zone 7 would actually grow in Zone 4. I was heartened when Agriculture and Agri-Food Canada published the results of its intensive evaluation of 160 grasses in over 80 species and 43 genera for the Northern Great Plains. Authors Davidson and Gobin at the Morden Research Centre in Manitoba provided the scientific evidence that proved there is indeed a wide range of low-maintenance grasses hardy enough to grow in cold and generally dry conditions. Ornamental grasses now enjoy one of the top perennial spots in the "best cultivar" charts of the Michigan State University annual floriculture industry survey. Although the Canadian industry does not yet conduct its own study, nurseries are experiencing the positive impact of the ornamental grass movement in Canadian gardening.

When I realized that local gardeners working in small spaces were hesitant to use ornamental grasses because of their heights — some more than 6 feet (1.8 m), I began to hybridize shorter grasses suitable for Ontario conditions. (This doesn't mean I don't recommend the tall grasses for a small garden, because I do and will continue to promote them as important specimen plants in even the smallest of spaces.)

Our first successes were *Miscanthus sinensis* 'Huron Sunrise' and 'Huron

Sunset.' They are unique for their flower colour — a deep burgundy, much darker than any of the other *Miscanthus* species available — and for their relatively low height. 'Huron Sunrise' grows to 4 feet (120 cm) and 'Huron Sunset' reaches 3 feet (90 cm).

'Huron Sunrise' and 'Huron Sunset' now thrive in our one-acre (.4-hectare) demonstration gardens. They grow in clay soil on land that for years served as stony fields for cattle. To the original barns and sheds we have added a number of hoop greenhouses as we have made the horticultural transition to a low-tech, family operation. What our demonstration gardens may lack in formal design unity they make up for in the variety of unique and challenging beds we are developing in shade, full sun, dry and wet conditions. Many of the 120 varieties of grass we now grow play significant and varied roles in these beds and perennial borders.

The new prominence of grasses in garden design is one small step in a long history of ornamental and practical plant-growing that goes back millenia.

North American gardening history began thousands of years ago when aboriginal people broke soil to plant vegetable seeds, gathered wild rice or processed cereal grain grasses like corn, wheat, rye or oats for sustenance. Other lovely grasses, like bamboo, played practical roles in early construction as well as ornamental roles in Chinese and Japanese garden art.

Ornamental grasses were somewhat popular in the early years of the twentieth century in North America, but by the 1940s they had fallen into a state of sad cliché in the over-present pampas grasses of suburban landscapes. It wasn't until plant breeders and designers like Karl Foerster, Kurt Bluemel, Wolfgang Oehme, Jim Van Sweden and Piet Oudolf came on the scene that ornamental grasses regained prominence. In a move away from the old horticultural

# introduction

schools of mastery and imitation and toward gardening in harmony with nature, this group has established its own natural school of design. They have also placed grass gardening squarely in the heart of today's environmental movement.

Although gardening in a natural style has never been easier than it is with perennial ornamental grasses, they are still relatively unknown. Many garden centres carry somewhat limited selections and when these are displayed beside other bedding plants or perennials the withered-looking shoots of potted baby grasses can sometimes look like ugly ducklings.

Remarkably adaptable and resilient, however, they prove to be hardy, relatively disease and pest free and very low maintenance. Most thrive in the sun, but they flourish in a wide range of light, soil, climate and moisture conditions. Now that these traits are better known, ornamental grasses are being planted in public and private gardens,

golf courses and parks. They are recognized for their beauty and ability to attract butterflies and birds. And they are also being pressed into environmental service in large-scale erosion control, water purification and naturalizing projects.

When Catherine and I married in 1991 we started the grass business and began planning to move home to Kincardine where our parents, families and many dear old friends lived.

In our dream was an old home on land with some character, a few acres for greenhouses, some sturdy outbuildings and room for offices and a classroom. In 1997 we bought that farm. Our plans didn't include writing a book on gardening with ornamental grasses, but it became obvious that with my photographs and practical knowledge and Catherine's writing skills we had everything we needed to produce *Grass Scapes*. In the summer of 2000 we rolled up our sleeves and started to work on it in earnest.

*Grass Scapes* is an introduction to gardening with hardy ornamental grasses. It is written for gardeners at all levels of practice and shows how a simple understanding of basic grass shapes, sizes, colours and functions can open the door to gardening confidently with hardy ornamental grasses. We hope you will use it to bring these beautiful, versatile and useful plants into your own gardens and communities.

## Hardiness Zones

In grass hardiness tests we have found that a number of Zone 7 varieties grow well in Zone 4 if there is good snow cover. Grasses identified as Zone 7 plants grow easily into Zone 6 and sometimes right into Zone 4 when deep snow cover protects the ground from frost. Keep in mind that zone ratings are not always a perfect gauge for determining winter hardiness. In some southern locations a particular plant may die in winter while the same variety, snug under a blanket of snow, may be fine farther north.

Gardeners in Canada and the U.S. can refer to their appropriate Hardiness Zone Maps, which are based on average climatic conditions of each area. These take into account minimum winter temperatures, length of the frost-free period, summer rainfall, maximum temperatures, snow cover, January rainfall and maximum wind speed.

Although the Canadian and U.S. maps overlap some-what, they are not the same. The Canadian map has nine zones — from the Yukon to temperate B.C. The U.S. map has 11 zones, ranging from Alaska to tropical Hawaii. The recent Agriculture Canada map also includes significant subzones and incorporates the impact of elevation — especially important in western Canada and the US. Readers who have access to the Internet can visit the Web site. Each site is hyperlinked so that visitors can type the name of their community and zoom into excellent close-ups.

These maps offer a guideline, but year-to-year variations in weather and gardening techniques can impact on plant survival in any particular location. Wise gardeners, therefore, still rely on local gardening expertise and word of mouth — as we have since the beginning of gardening time.

**Canada**  http://sis.agr.gc.ca/cansis/nsdb/climate/hardiness/intro.html
**U.S.**  http://www.usna.usda.gov/Hardzone/ushzmap.html

# about grasses

Ornamental grasses challenge some of the traditional approaches to garden design, but they bring a new sense of life and drama to the garden. Perhaps their most exceptional quality — the one that cannot be drawn onto any plan or illustrated on any garden centre tag — is animation. Even the most subtle of breezes will create a virtual ballet of movement and sound. Grasses in motion can whisper like silk, rustle like satin, whistle like wind or wail like a winter storm.

Playfulness with light is another outstanding attribute. From dawn to dusk, the changing light transforms a grass garden's character, mood and form — intensifying foliage and flower shape, heightening colour or tossing the grasses into dramatic silhouette.

The first step in using grasses is to become familiar with how they grow — from their roots to their flowers — and how to care for them.

# root systems and growth habit

True ornamental grasses have two distinct growing habits — clump-forming and spreading.

## clumpers

Clumpers grow in lateral shoots from their base, keeping the plant compact. They are slow, steady growers and these grasses are the ones used most in beds and borders as accents, in mosaic plantings, for layering or in mass plantings.

**Leymus
arenarius glauca**
(blue lime grass)

has wonderful
metallic blue
flowers. Plant it in
containers only; it
is very invasive
and is used prima-
rily for erosion
control. It is usually
found around the
edges of lakes and
streams, particularly
in dry, sandy
conditions.

## runners

Runners, or spreading grasses, spread
by above-ground horizontal roots called
*stolons*, which can produce new plants
at each node or by underground rhizomes. Some grasses with aggressive
spreading root systems, like *Spartina
pectinata* (prairie cord grass) and
*Phalaris arundinacea* (ribbon grass), can
vary from highly invasive to moderately
invasive and may be used successfully
with a bit of attention and special care.

Many people are put off when they
know that a grass has a spreading habit,
but invasive grasses play important
roles in bank establishment and erosion
control. They can be used in a garden
setting if they are kept in check with an
attentive eye and a good sharp spade or
as container plants.

# leaves, stems and flowers

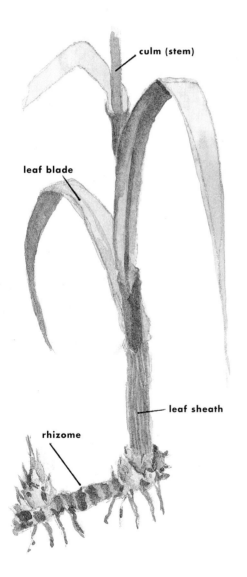

culm (stem)

leaf blade

leaf sheath

rhizome

## leaves

Each leaf is composed of three parts —
a vertical *sheath*, which grows from a
node and wraps around the stem; an
almost invisible *ligule*, which is a pro-
tective membrane of thin hairs at the
juncture of the sheath; and a *blade*, the
part of the leaf above the sheath.

The grass blade grows away from
the stem and is usually open and narrow
with parallel veins and a large median
vein called a *midrib*. *Miscanthus sinensis*
leaves range in width from $^1/_4$ to $^1/_2$ inch
(.6 to 1.2 cm) and have a distinctive and
prominent white midrib. The overall
height of a grass does not necessarily
determine the size of the leaves: the
bold, glossy leaves of *Hakonechloa macra*
(hakone grass) are the same width as
those of the very tall *M. sinensis*
'Gracillimus' (maiden grass).

Grass has an unusual way of growing
that contributes to its survival. Most
plants grow from the tips of their leaves

**Chasmanthium
latifolium**

and branches. Anyone who has cared
for a lawn will know that grass has two
distinct growing points — at the base
of each leaf and just above each growth
node on the stem. This growth pattern
means that grass can keep on growing
even after cutting, cropping by animals,
or even fire.

## stems

Most grass stems, or *culms,* are herba-
ceous, hollow and cylindrical or slightly
flattened. The rounded shape is one
way to differentiate them from sedges,
most of which have three-angled stems.
(The stems of sedges are also pithy, not
hollow like grasses.) The leaves are
attached at swollen joints called nodes.
The *internode* is the stem part between
the nodes.

**Calamagrotsis x acutiflora** 'Karl Foerster'

# flowers

What we call grass flowers are actually a complex group of structures, usually arranged in clusters on a stem, which together are called an *inflorescence*. The three basic flower types of grass flowers are a *spike*, a *raceme* and a *panicle*.

inflorescence

A *spike* is elongated; the individual spikelets have no stalks and are attached directly to the central axis or *rachis*. *Pennisetum setaceum* 'Rubrum' (red fountain grass) is an example.

A *raceme* is more open; the spikelets are suspended from the *rachis* on short stalks. An example is *Chasmanthium latifolium* (northern sea oats), with tiny, oat-like stems.

**spikelet**         **floret**

**spike** *Pennisetum setaceum* 'Rubrum' (red fountain grass) and *Alopecurus pratensis* (yellow foxtail)

**raceme** *Phalaris arundinacea* (ribbon grass) and *Chasmanthium latifolium* (northern sea oats)

**panicle** *Bromus inermis* (smooth brome)

## flowers (continued)

A *panicle* is multi-branched and very open; stalks branch out from the rachis and stemmed spikelets are attached to these stalks. *Deschampsia cespitosa* (tufted hair grass) is an example.

Some flowers are a compound of panicles and racemes. Together panicles and racemes create the magnificent plumes of *Miscanthus sinensis* flowers.

Awns are slender, often silky, sometimes stiff bristles attached to the bract of a grass flower. Awns create the beautiful plumes on grasses like *Hordeum jubatum*.

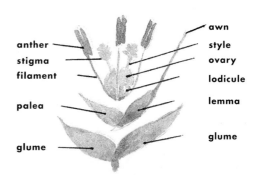

anther — style
stigma — ovary
filament — lodicule
palea — lemma
glume — glume
awn

**compound of panicles and racemes**
*Miscanthus sinensis*

**Miscanthus sinensis 'Sarabande'**

# grass forms

For our purposes we divide grasses into six general structures: upright, upright arching, arching, upright divergent, mounded and tufted.

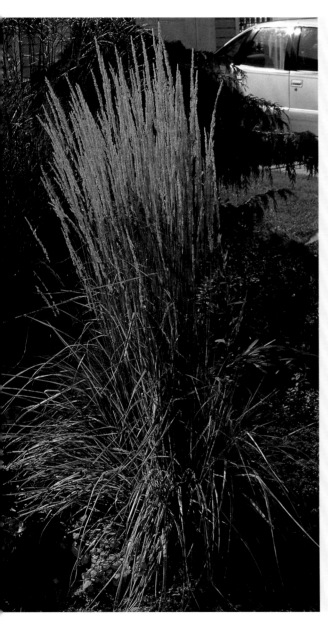

**Calamagrostis** x **acutiflora 'Overdam'**

## upright

grasses come in a variety of heights, but tall, medium or small, they all provide linear exclamation points in a garden design. The foliage and flowers of the medium-high *Calamagrostis arundinacea* var. *brachytricha* (fall-blooming reed grass) grows from a tidy clumping base of 30 inches to 3 feet (75 to 90 cm) in flower. Arrow-straight, with upright vertical leaves and erect, slender flower heads, it works equally well as an individual specimen or in mass plantings. *Imperata cylindrica* 'Red Baron' (Japanese blood grass) is small at 16 inches (40 cm), but this intensely red decorative is another popular upright grass.

A six-year-old *Calamagrostis* 'Overdam'. This grass is hardy, very erect and sturdy. It has a vigorous clumping habit and grows to about 30 inches (75 cm) in height. The leaves are about ¹/₂ inch (1.2 cm) wide. Flowers are pink, turning blonde by September. 'Overdam' is a good companion plant for *Miscanthus floridulus* or the amazing red *Panicum* 'Warrior.'

**upright**                                   **upright arching**

## upright arching

foliage springs from the base, ascends
stiffly and vertically, then falls in a
fountain of arcs from the top. The low-
growing burgundy annual *Pennisetum
setaceum* 'Eaton Canyon' (miniature red
fountain grass) with bottlebrush-like
flowers, *Molinia caerulea* 'Variegata'
(variegated moor grass) and the stat-
uesque *Saccharum ravennae* (hardy
pampas grass) are all good examples.
*Arundo donax* (Giant reed) and
*Chasmanthium latifolium* (northern sea
oats) are two of the tallest grass varieties.
In full flower, magnificent *C. latifolium*
flower heads droop languidly well
above their foliage.

Native to wet prairies and marshes from Maine
to the great plains, the tall variegated *Spartina
pectinata* 'Aureomarginata' (prairie cord grass)
is stately, upright and arching. Its golden flowers
in late July or early August look great near ponds.

**Miscanthus sinensis 'Gracillimus'**
accenting a garden bench in a small townhouse garden

**Hordeum jubatum**
(foxtail barley)

# arching

varieties include the popular *Miscanthus sinensis,* which has over 60 named cultivars, each charming in its own way. *M. sinensis* foliage grows vertically at slight angles from its clumping base; an outstanding example is 'Huron Sentinel' (Huron Sentinel maiden grass). This new introduction is a superb specimen in a bed or border. Alone it is like a solitary royal guardsman; in a mass planting, it is like an entire regiment at attention.

The beautifully arching *Hordeum jubatum* (foxtail barley) grows to 18 inches (45 cm) high and 2 feet (60 cm) wide at maturity, with a purplish flower. It makes a good naturalizing plant as its seed is viable and grows easily. *Lupine* and *Penstemon grandiflorus* (beardtongue) are good companions.

**upright divergent**

## upright divergent

foliage grows up and out from its base at a forty-degree angle in a stiffly vertical manner, like a slightly open fan. The multi-purpose beauty *Calamagrostis* x *acutiflora* 'Karl Foerster' (feather reed grass) is a fine example. The stately native prairie variety *Andropogon gerardii* (big bluestem) is another.

Spectacular *Molinia caerulea* ssp. *arundinacea* 'Skyracer' in flower can be up to 8 feet (2.4 m) high from a base clump of about 3 feet (90 cm) at ground level. In late autumn its leaves are a rich golden yellow. The delicate panicles appear in July in glorious sprays of rich purple or bronze. In autumn, the flower matures to a subtle blonde. 'Skyracer' has a strong yet graceful sculptural form and lasts for years with minimal maintenance. It grows best in full sun with plenty of moisture but will tolerate dry conditions as well.

**Molinia caerulea** ssp. **arundinacea** 'Skyracer'

**mounded**

## mounded

grass forms have foliage that cascades over lower leaves. They are generally small to medium in height. There are relatively few varieties that take this form, but mounded grasses are good choices for adding texture, punctuating beds and creating borders. Good decorative grasses are *Hakonechloa macra* 'Aureola' (golden variegated hakone grass) and *Helictotrichon sempervirens* (blue oat grass). Mounded varieties are great companions for taller grasses because they can be used effectively to cover the unsightly "bare legs" that often appear at the base of taller varieties as a season progresses.

*Carex muskingumensis* (palm sedge), a North America native, grows in sunny areas and dappled shade to a height of 2 feet (60 cm). It needs moist soil. Good bog garden companion plants are *Eupatorium maculatum* (joe pye weed) and *Eupatorium perfoliatum* (boneset).

**Carex muskingumensis** (palm sedge)

**Festuca amethystina** 'Superba'

# tufted

grasses have short, thin and spiky upright leaves. There are relatively few named varieties that take this form. Two examples are fine-textured grasses like the small *Festuca glauca* 'Boulder Blue' (blue fescue) and *Deschampsia cespitosa* (tufted hair grass). *Festuca amethystina* 'Superba' has lovely, rainbow-coloured flower stems above bright blue leaves.

The tufted *Helictotrichon sempervirens* (blue oat grass) pictured here in the right foreground has been a best-selling perennial grass for a number of years. Very compact, with a striking metallic blue colour, this versatile plant grows to about 16 inches (40 cm) across and 2 feet (60 cm) high with a 46-inch (1.2-m) flower height. It prospers in all conditions, from dry to wet and sun to shade. Its fine texture complements many different plants. In the garden we like the contrast of brown-leafed *Eupatorium* 'Chocolate' or heavily textured *Sedum* 'Autumn Joy.'

**Helictotrichon sempervirens** (blue oat grass)

# how grasses are named

All plants have botanical names, and these are the standard for identification.

**Miscanthus sinensis** 'Huron Sunrise'

They help alleviate confusion that can be caused by the many common names that inevitably attach themselves to well-loved plants. When I write about grasses I place the common name, which is usually the easiest to remember, in brackets after the botanical name. Botanical names have two basic parts: the *genus* and the *species*. The genus represents a number of species sharing distinctive characteristics and is always capitalized and in italics. The species name is also in italics but is not capitalized. (Note that the plural of genus is "genera" and that in some horticultural texts you may run into the term "specific epithet" for species.)

In nature there are many minor variations within species and these can be designated by subspecies or varieties (abbreviated as ssp. and var.). These terms are not italicized.

Breeders cultivate specific characteristics in grasses and these are called cultivars (shortened from cultivated variety) and given names that are enclosed in single quotation marks.

**Molinia caerulea** ssp. **arundinacea** 'Skyracer'

The chart below compares *Miscanthus sinensis* and *Molinia caerulea*.

| Plant Name | Miscanthus sinensis 'Huron Sunrise' | Molinia caerulea ssp. arundinacea 'Skyracer' |
|---|---|---|
| Genus | Miscanthus | Molinia |
| Species (or specific epithet) | sinensis | caerulea |
| Variety or subspecies | N/A | arundinacea |
| Cultivar | 'Huron Sunrise' | 'Skyracer' |
| Common name | (Huron silver grass) | (Tall purple moor grass) |

# cultivation and maintenance

Ornamental grasses thrive in the kind of soils found in most gardens — a combination of clay and sand amended with perculite, vermiculite and humus obtained from grass or leaf mulch, peat moss, straw and compost.

Grasses do not require high fertility and adapt well to all soil conditions, from sand to heavy clay. In clay they usually take an extra year to mature. In sandy soil, with less moisture, they tend to be smaller in height.

The efficient fibrous root systems of grasses make them especially drought-resistant. Occasionally, in very wet seasons, grass foliage can succumb to rust, but that problem is easily solved by giving the plants more space and breathing room. Ornamental grasses provide all-season interest except during the few weeks in spring when we trim them. Then borders and beds look polka-dotted with giant pincushions. This prickly phenomenon lasts only two or three weeks as new shoots begin to appear almost immediately. It's a good diversionary tactic to cut grasses back when their colourful spring bulb neighbours are in bloom.

Grasses are either warm- or cool-season species, depending on their periods of active growth. Warm-season grasses, like *Miscanthus sinensis,* grow roots in warm weather. Cool-season grasses like *Holcus mollis* grow roots in spring and autumn and sleep during hot weather.

## dividing grasses

The grasses covered in this book are mostly perennials, so treat them as you do all others — divide them when they are too large or when the centres die out and become unsightly.

In cooler climates it is best to divide plants in the spring. We keep it simple by doing all the dividing in spring. Most climatic zones do not have a long enough growing season for warm-season grasses — those that thrive in fine weather — to root properly before the onset of winter if divided in autumn.

When dividing grasses, dig around the plant with a shovel or spade about 6 inches (15 cm) away from the clump. Then dig under the clump and lift it out of the hole. Plunge two digging forks, back to back, into the root ball.

**dividing grasses** dig around the plant with a shovel or spade about 6 inches (15 cm) away from the clump.

### dividing tips

- Inspect large grass plants in fall to select grasses for division.

- Divide both warm- and cool-season grasses in spring to keep it simple.

- Use sharp, strong shovels, spades and digging forks.

- Wear good footwear.

- Don't be timid about dividing the roots. Grasses can take it.

- Don't dig any closer than 6 inches (15 cm) from a clump.

- Dig under the root mass, rather than trying to pry the root ball upwards. This could break your spade and shovel handles.

- Plant new divisions immediately, using the guidelines in the planting section. Roots should never be exposed to the sun.

### dividing grasses (continued)

Some mature clumps require a good jump on the forks in order to penetrate the root mass. Depending on the size of the plant and allowing for a 4-inch (20-cm) root mass in each new division, you can make two, four or eight plants.

Gently spread the roots apart.

Place the grass in the prepared hole and half-fill the hole with soil.

## planting grasses

Ornamental grasses can be purchased in garden centres, box stores or through mail-order nurseries that specialize in grasses. Normally they are sold in 5-gallon (20 L), 2- gallon (8 L) or 1-gallon (4 L) (the most popular) sizes. Some mail-order nurseries sell bare-root clumps.

Before planting, do your research. It is important to know the size of ornamental grasses at maturity. Some can grow into giants. Know your site and make sure the new plant you choose is suited to the location. Though exceptions exist, there are general guidelines for spacing. Small grasses need 1 square foot (.09 m²) of room to grow; medium grasses may require 2 to 3 square feet (.18 to .27 m²), depending on the actual height. Tall grasses should have lots of room — 4 square feet (.36 m²) for giants like *Arundo donax*.

# cutting back

Since we enjoy our grasses throughout winter and we like to spread the gardening workload, we don't cut them back until early spring. Spring varies from area to area, so monitor the grasses and cut them back before new growth starts.

## planting tips

- Plant in spring, even though some grass varieties will not yet be starting to grow.

- Water the plant well before planting.

- Dig an area three times larger than the size of the pot.

- Amend the soil with peat moss, manure or compost if necessary.

- Remove the plant from the pot. If the root mass fills the pot completely, gently spread the roots apart.

- Place the grass in the prepared hole and half-fill the hole with soil.

- Water well.

- Fill the hole with soil and compress with your hands.

- Be sure the crown is at or just above soil level.

- Don't baby new grasses by overwatering or overfeeding. (They are tough.)

We use a very simple formula to determine how much to cut back. If a grass grows under 3 feet (90 cm) in height, cut it back to 2 inches (5 cm); if a grass grows over 3 feet (90 cm) cut it cut back to 4 inches (10 cm).

We have tried many tools for cutting back — pruners, hedge clippers, electric hedge clippers and weed whippers. We finally settled on a gas-powered hedge trimmer because of the number of plants we grow. Choose the tool that best suits your needs.

In the past we removed grass clippings to the compost heap, but recently we have started to leave the clippings right in the beds. We turn them into mulch by cutting the stalks into sections, snipping the stems off 6 inches (15 cm) at a time until we reach the desired height.

### tips for cutting back

- Cut grasses back in early spring, before new growth starts.

- Use newly sharpened and oiled tools.

- Don't be afraid to cut grasses back aggressively. Cut those less than 3 feet (90 cm) back to 2 inches (5 cm) and those over 3 feet (90 cm) back to 4 inches (10 cm)

- Mulch or compost leaves and stems.

- Never cut new growth.

# working with colour

One of the first prints we had framed when we started working with ornamental grasses was *The Tangled Garden* by Canadian Group of Seven painter J.E.H. MacDonald (1873–1932). It still hangs above the fireplace in the main room of our house, reminding us of the challenges of the work and, in amber, green and red, complementing the colourful grass gardens visible from the two large windows.

Visual artists and artisans have turned to nature for their colour inspiration and dyes for centuries. Colour can express a mood, provide a background, act as an accent, suggest harmony, give a sense of scale and create the illusion of space and perspective. In a famous 1846 essay, the French poet Baudelaire claimed that nature couldn't make a mistake when it comes to colour because form and colour in nature are one. He believed that true colourists couldn't make mistakes either, because they seem to know by instinct the tone values, the results of mixing and the science of counter-point. "That's why they can create harmony with 20 different reds," he explained.

The key word in ornamental grass colour is subtlety. In spring and summer, grasses usually play supporting roles behind more showy shrubs, perennials and annuals. To the uninitiated they may seem like the supporting cast for peonies, roses, delphiniums and other divas. Experienced ornamental grass gardeners, however, know that grass colours range from greens, blues, reds, yellows and browns to white and even black. Variegated grasses are adorned with whites, ivories and creams. The spring and summer garden may have a vibrant colour chorus of funky, lime green *Carex albula* 'Frosty Curls,' a powdery blue *Helictotrichon sempervirens*, an intense burgundy *Pennisetum setaceum* 'Rubrum,' a burgundy

*Panicum virgatum* 'Huron Solstice,' and a polished bronze *Carex buchananii*. Not only that, but leaves, stems, foliage, seed heads and flower heads can all be different colours. Grasses like *Festuca amethystina*, for example, change dra-matically through the season. Its stem is as important as the leaf and flower head in colour selection.

When the summer garden relaxes into autumn, grasses really come into their own. Flower heads are a parade of feathery bonnets and tasseled caps in purples, burgundies, pinks, bronzes, coppers and silvers. Once open and primed to disperse, the seeds take on a subtler but no less dazzling range of hues — gossamer blondes, ethereal golds and diaphanous platinums. A group planting of burgundy-flowered *Miscanthus sinensis* 'Huron Sunrise,' *Panicum virgatum* 'Heavy Metal' and variegated varieties like *Molina caerulea* 'Variegata' can really shine as the days shorten and the quality of light changes.

green          blue          red          pink

A fabulous combination is *Saccharum ravennae* with its towering, spear-like flowers, a medium-sized *Miscanthus sinensis* 'Huron Sunrise' and a small *Deschampsia cespitosa*, which, when in flower, wears a halo of the finest lace. To complete the picture add autumn lingerers like *Athyrium niponicum* 'Pictum' (Japanese painted fern), *Eupatorium rugosum* 'Chocolate,' delphiniums and unbridled cosmos. Almost any grass will dance with a dowager *Rudbeckia* 'Lacinata' or hardy chrysanthemums in autumn. This is also the time when the almost purple *Chasmanthium latifolium*, burgundy *Imperata cylindrica* 'Red Baron' and pink-suffused *Miscanthus sinensis* 'Huron Sunrise' form a vibrant trio. In autumn a crimson *M.* 'Purpurascens' creates a magnificent counterpoint to the golden yellows of *Pennisetum alopecuroides* and *P. alopecuroides* 'Hameln.'

Though it may seem daunting at first, with some practice and observation designing with the colour subtleties of ornamental grasses can be as rewarding as any other artistic or decorative endeavour. The "Grasses at a Glance" section at the back of this book, which profiles over a hundred hardy varieties, will help, for the variations are countless. Whether it is several grasses of one colour in a monochromatic scheme, a dominant colour with a range of complementary colours, or a selection of harmonizers like blues, reds and yellows, ornamental grasses are a colourist's dream.

# summer colour

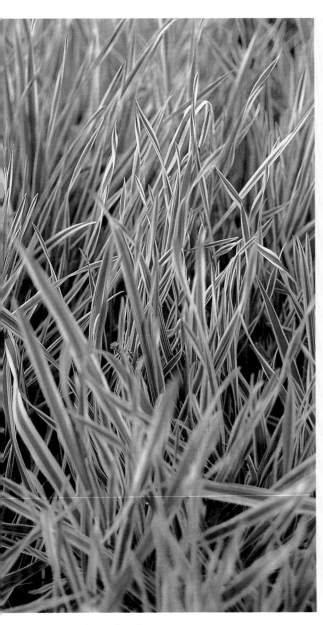

## white variegated

A very young, low-growing *Holcus mollis* 'Albo-variegatus.' Although this small grass looks somewhat like the more sparsely structured *Arrhenatherum elatius* 'Variegatus' (bulbous oat grass), it is not used much in garden design yet. 'Albo-variegatus' is a great ground cover. It mats out first thing in the spring and maintains fullness throughout the growing season if in a shaded area with cool temperatures. It fades away and almost seems to die in too much sun, but as soon as the weather cools downs it bounces back. It grows to only 6 inches (15 cm) in height but in two to three years it spreads to about 1 foot (30 cm).

### more summer whites

*Arrhenatherum elatius* ssp. *bulbosum* 'Variegatus'
*Arundo donax* 'Variegata'
*Calamagrostis* x *acutiflora* 'Overdam'
*Miscanthus sinensis* 'Cabaret'
*Miscanthus sinensis* 'Morning Light'
*Miscanthus sinensis* 'Variegatus'
*Pennisetum alopecuroides* 'Little Honey'
*Phalaris arundinacea* 'Picta'

**white** *Holcus mollis* 'Albo-variegatus'

## yellow

This vivid *Carex elata* 'Bowles' Golden' with intense yellow foliage adds a pleasing upright structure to any garden. It is relatively slow growing, but given rich, well-drained soil that is high in organic matter it will grow more quickly and display more luxuriant foliage. It performs in a range of conditions, from partial sun to shade. About 18" (45 cm) high, a mature clump can be 1 foot (30 cm) wide.

**more summer yellows**

*Alopecurus pratensis* 'Aureus'
*Hakonechloa macra* 'Aureola'
*Miscanthus sinensis* 'Huron Penetangore'
*Miscanthus sinensis* 'Little Zebra'
*Miscanthus sinensis* 'Puenktchen'
*Miscanthus sinensis* 'Strictus'
*Miscanthus sinensis* 'Zebrinus'
*Molinia caerulea* 'Variegata'

**yellow** *Carex elata* 'Bowles' Golden' planted with *Artemisia* 'Silver Brocade' and *Ophiopogon planiscapus* 'Niger.' This young planting shows an attractive yellow, silver and black combination.

summer colour

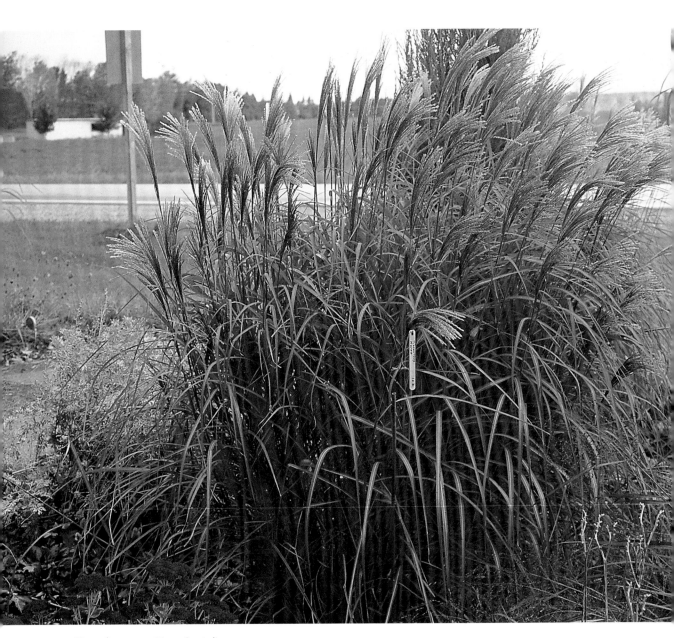

**green** *Miscanthus sinensis* 'Huron Sentinel'

## green

*Miscanthus sinensis* 'Huron Sentinel' flowers appear in September, bringing the overall height to 5 feet (1.5 m). As the season advances the plumes change from red to deep bronze. When late summer and autumn winds play, it performs a stunning dance number with an equally tall-growing *Rudbeckia* 'Laciniata.' *Panicum virgatum* planted in front creates a pleasing layered effect.

**more summer greens**

*Calamagrostis* x *acutiflora* 'Karl Foerster'

*Miscanthus sinensis* 'Huron Blush'

*Miscanthus sinensis* 'Huron Sunrise'

*Miscanthus sinensis* 'Huron Sunset'

*Pennisetum alopecuroides* 'Little Bunny'

*Pennisetum alopecuroides* 'Moudry'

*Saccharum ravennae*

summer colour

## blue

A recent introduction, powder blue *Festuca glauca* 'Boulder Blue' is about the same size as *F. glauca* 'Sea Urchin,' although it doesn't flower as well. It is a real eye-catcher, however, when planted with *Carex buchananii* (bronze leather leaf sedge) and *Sedum* 'Vera Jameson.' 'Boulder Blue' tolerates very dry conditions and thrives in heavy or light soil.

**more summer blues**

*Festuca glauca* 'Boulder Blue'

*Festuca glauca* 'Elijah Blue'

*Festuca glauca* 'Sea Urchin'

*Helictotrichon sempervirens*

*Koeleria glauca*

*Panicum virgatum* 'Heavy Metal'

*Panicum virgatum* 'Prairie Sky'

**Blue** *Festuca glauca* 'Boulder Blue'

## red

The vibrant red of this translucent, light-rooted *Imperata cylindrica* 'Red Baron' intensifies gradually until the first heavy frosts, when it turns brown. It will grow in partial shade but for the best colour performance it needs full sun in protected spots near rocks.

For astounding contrast try *Imperata cylindrica* 'Red Baron' with *Lamium* 'White Nancy.'

**more summer reds**
*Panicum virgatum* 'Shenandoah'
*Pennisetum setaceum* 'Rubrum'

**red** *Imperata cylindrica* 'Red Baron'

# autumn colour

## pink (variegated)

**More autumn pinks**
*Phalaris arundinacea* 'Feesey's Form'
*Miscanthus sinensis* 'Variegatus'
*Miscanthus sinensis* 'Cabaret'

**pink** *Phalaris arundinacea* 'Feesey's Form' with Iris in an Edmonton garden.

## red

A large stand of about 100 *Miscanthus* 'Purpurascens' (flame grass) in Kitchener, Ontario. 'Purpurascens' gets its name from its autumn foliage colour. It was selected by German nurseryman Dr. Hans Simon in the 1960s and has since proved to have the most reliable red-orange autumn colour of any *Miscanthus* species grown in Canada. The handsome, silver white, compact flower heads are more erect than most *Miscanthus* species and in Ontario appear relatively early, in late August or early September. Just over 5 feet (1.5 metres) tall to the tops of the flowers, its relatively small stature makes it ideal for use in more intimate gardens. A planting of three of these grasses in a smaller garden makes a great backdrop for *Rudbeckia fulgida* 'Goldsturm.'

**more autumn reds**

*Imperata cylindrica* 'Red Baron'
*Panicum virgatum* 'Heavy Metal'
*Panicum virgatum* 'Warrior'

**Red** *Miscanthus* 'Purpurascens'

autumn colour

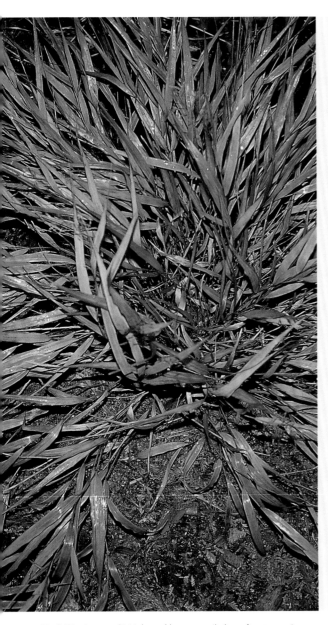

## red (variegated)

*Hakonechloa macra* (hakone forest grass) at its elegant best under a cedar tree in our garden. Its arching bamboo-like leaves are a lovely bronze in autumn. It grows to 1 foot (30 cm) high and 2 feet (60 cm) wide. A versatile groundcover, it resembles rolling waves when animated by wind. Plant it under a leaf canopy of *Hosta* for a lovely layered structure. *H. macra* flourishes in shaded areas in moist or dry conditions.

**more autumn reds**
*Hakonechloa macra 'Aureola'*
*Panicum virgatum 'Rehbraun'*

**Red (Variegated)** *Hakonechloa macra* (hakone forest grass)

## bright yellow

A graceful *Chasmanthium latifolium* (northern sea oats). Clump-forming and upright, it grows from 4 to 5 feet (1.2 to 1.5 m) in height. It is one of the few varieties we grow that produces viable seed. The seeds germinate where they fall and are easily identified when they start growing in very early spring. *C. latifolium* is especially interesting because it has two colour phases in autumn. Its yellow oat-like flower heads, which look like flattened, one-sided silk tassels, bow elegantly from arching terminal branches throughout the season. The yellow foliage, however, turns purple with frost. Plant this fine-leafed grass near a large-leafed hydrangea for a spectacular autumn effect.

**More autumn yellows**

*Molinia caerulea* ssp. *arundinacea* 'Skyracer'
*Panicum virgatum*
*Pennisetum alopecuroides*
*Pennisetum alopecuroides* 'Hameln'

**bright yellow** *Chasmanthium latifolium* (northern sea oats)

autumn colour

**bronze** *Schizachyrium scoparium* (little bluestem)

## bronze

The North American native *Schizachyrium scoparium* (little bluestem) in Niagara Park's Botanical Gardens. A fiery red in autumn it grows naturally on hillsides and meadows and can be used in the flower border or for naturalizing. It grows about 2 feet (60 cm) high and wide. Tiny, translucent flowers are produced along the upper two-thirds of its stems in late September. It needs good drainage with a lot of sun. It has a tendency to self-seed.

### more autumn bronzes

*Miscanthus sinensis* 'Huron Sentinel'
*Miscanthus sinensis* 'Graziella'
*Saccharum ravennae* (formerly *Erianthus ravennae*)

# winter colour

## blonde

*Miscanthus sinensis* 'Gracillimus'
*Miscanthus sinensis* 'Silberfeder'
*Miscanthus sinensis* 'Grosse Fontäne'
*Miscanthus sinensis* 'Malepartus'
*Panicum virgatum* 'Heavy Metal'
*Panicum virgatum* 'Warrior'
*Pennisetum alopecuroides* 'Hameln'

## bronze

*Carex* 'Buchananii'
*Hakonechloa macra*
*Pennisetum alopecuroides* and *Chasmanthium latifolium*
*Schizachyrium scoparium*

## blue

*Helictotrichon sempervirens*

# special conditions

Many visual artists have celebrated gardens with paints, textiles and glass. Poets, essayists and novelists have placed the ideal garden as a central metaphor in their works. But most of us work in ordinary patches where growing conditions are not ideal. And most of us cherish the magic of serendipity, bungling coincidence and dreams — realized or not — that personalize our garden spaces.

The following pages address a universe that includes deserts, scrublands and rock, patches of land beside sun-stealing high-rise buildings, dense woodland, bush, shaded valleys and long, cold winters.

# winter

Before we introduced ornamental grasses, our winter garden was a naked shadow of its charmed summer self.

**Miscanthus sinensis** 'Huron Sunrise' in summer

We delighted in the lacy branches of the old oaks and maples against the sky and depended on the birch trees in the front garden for their bright bark. The spruce gave us a bit of blue; glossy wide-leafed hostas and mock holly added some green, other evergreen shapes and shades threw in some variation. But ornamental grasses have trans-formed our winter landscape.

The foliage, plumes and tassels capture the sun magnificently on a sparkling white background. Freezing rain turns every leaf and stem into a glass wonderland. Silhouetted against the low winter light, grasses are almost free of colour, creating a monochromatic moving picture amid the ruins of summer annuals and perennials.

Whether upright divergent, mounded or arching, ornamental grass archi-tecture is most apparent and splendid in winter.

There is no better group of plants to highlight seasonal glories than grasses. *Miscanthus sinensis* 'Huron Sunrise' in summer and winter.

**Miscanthus sinensis** 'Huron Sunrise' in winter

**Carex buchananii**

*Carex buchananii* pokes through the first snow like a four-dimensional line drawing. This petite tufted sedge with thin round leaves and curled tips is 2 feet (60 cm) high and 14 inches (36 cm) wide.

*Hakonechloa macra* is one of the most elegant of groundcovers. Its bamboo-like 1-foot (30-cm) arching leaves grow in 2-feet (60-cm) mounds.

**Hakonechloa macra**

# winter

**Helictotrichon sempervirens** (blue oat grass)

A group of 10 *Helictotrichon sempervirens* (blue oat grass) accent the junction of two pathways in an Exeter, Ontario, planting. The metallic blue leaves of summer, now a jubilant winter yellow, give texture to the snowy landscape.

With a tall Clumner spruce, the finely structured *Miscanthus sinensis* 'Gracillimus' provides a flourish of blonde contrast and seasonal flamboyance.

**Miscanthus sinensis** 'Gracillimus'

**Miscanthus sinensis** 'Silberfeder'

*Miscanthus sinensis* 'Silberfeder' is more upright in structure and has wider leaves than 'Gracillimus.' Its winter halo of downy white plumes are superb snow catchers.

A 6-foot (1.8-m) snow-bound *Miscanthus sinensis* 'Malepartus' arches under the weight of snow. This robust, upright plant with a 5-foot (1.5-m) girth turns silver blonde in winter.

**Miscanthus sinensis** 'Malepartus'

# winter

**Panicum virgatum** 'Warrior'

The open, arching structure of *Panicum virgatum* 'Warrior' brings animation to winter settings. It grows to 4 feet (1.2 m) across.

*Pennisetum alopecuroides* with *Chasmanthium latifolium* in the background. The structural delicacy of this medium-sized grass transforms to a crystal fountain in snow and frost.

**Pennisetum alopecuroides**
(*Chasmanthium latifolium* in background)

**Pennisetum alopecuroides** 'Hameln'

An elegant *Pennisetum alopecuroides* 'Hameln' arches in front of a snow-covered rock installation.

Medium-sized *Schizachyrium scoparium* (little bluestem) is a great naturalizing plant that gives contrasting texture and colour to this planting of juniper.

**Schizachyrium scoparium** (little bluestem)

# wetlands

Wetlands occur in low-lying areas near freshwater lakes, ponds, streams and rivers, or near salt water in coastal areas.

**Miscanthus floridulus** in wet conditions

In wetlands, the water is usually at, above, or just below the land surface. Only plants that don't mind having wet feet thrive under these conditions.

Besides providing important wildlife habitat, wetlands help prevent flooding and clean contaminated water through natural filtering processes. All of the ornamental grasses in this section thrive in damp, moist conditions near ponds and streams. Some even do well in extreme conditions, like bogs and marshes. Most of the plants here will grow in drier soil too, but they behave differently without moisture. In dry conditions, *Miscanthus floridulus*, for example, will grow only 5 feet (1.5 m) high with a few green leaves among a number of dry-looking brown leaves. With plenty of moisture it can grow from 12 to 14 feet (3.7 to 4.4 m) high with an abundance of rich green leaves well into autumn.

**Miscanthus floridulus** in dry conditions

**Arundo donax**

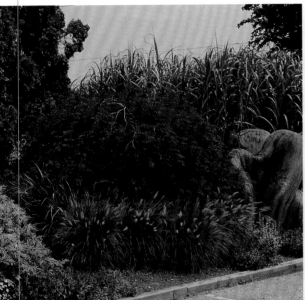

*Arundo donax* is a heavy drinker. The wetter and hotter it is the better it grows. It grows up to 14 feet (3.6 m) and can get much taller in a hot, wet season. Here it is pictured with *Pennisetum setaceum* 'Rubrum' at Waterloo Gardens in Philadelphia.

*Miscanthus sinensis* 'Huron Sunrise' and *Miscanthus sinensis* 'Variegatus' side by side in moist, heavy clay soil. Most *Miscanthus* species, particularly the larger-leafed ones, do well in both moist and dry conditions. Try planting these in a moist spot with the magnificent *Ligularia* 'The Rocket.'

**Miscanthus sinensis** 'Huron Sunrise' and
**Miscanthus sinensis** 'Variegatus'

# wetlands

*Miscanthus sinensis* 'Strictus' (porcupine grass) at Niagara Parks Botanical Gardens, Niagara Falls, Ontario. With its yellow horizontal striping, height of 5 feet (1.5 m) and width of 4 feet (1.2 m), 'Strictus' makes a great specimen plant. It creates magic when planted near long-flowering *Gaura lindheimeri* 'Whirling Butterflies' or 'Siskiyou Pink.'

**Miscanthus sinensis** 'Strictus' (porcupine grass)

A young *Molinia caerulea* ssp. arundinacea 'Skyracer' is already about 6 feet (1.8 m) tall in Kurt Bluemel's garden near Baltimore. *Molinia* species will grow in either moist or dry conditions. Planted with *Rodgersia pinnata* 'Superba,' with its larger leaf structure and pink flower spikes, the texture and colour of 'Skyracer' are electric.

**Molinia caerulea** ssp. **arundinacea** 'Skyracer'

# wetlands

**Panicum virgatum** 'Warrior'

*Panicum virgatum* 'Warrior' has a purple leaf and a lovely metallic flower that also turns purple in the autumn. It has an upright divergent habit and grows in moist conditions. 'Warrior' grows about 3 feet (90 cm) high and about 4 feet (1.2 m) wide. A good companion plant is *Kirengeshoma palmate* (waxbells), which has maple-like leaves and drooping yellow flowers in late summer.

*Phalaris arundinacea* 'Feesey's Form' provides good erosion control and makes a great container plant. We planted 300 one-gallon pots to stop water from washing out the eighteenth green at Islington Golf and Country Club in Toronto. 'Feesey's Form' is invasive and must be spaded each spring for control. It has a variegated white and green leaf with a line of pink in the white area. It grows from 2 to 3 feet (60 to 90 cm) tall and can spread to 5 feet (1.5 m) or more if not controlled.

**Phalaris arundinacea** 'Feesey's Form'

**Alopecurus pratensis** 'Aureus'

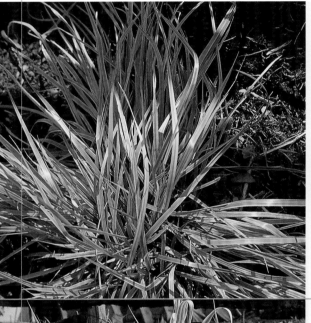

*Alopecurus pratensis* 'Aureus' has a yellow and green variegation and performs well in moist conditions, near ponds or streams.

A young stand of *Arundo donax* 'Variegata' at 6 to 9 feet (1.8 to 2.7 m) tall and 2 to 3 feet (60 to 90 cm) wide. This grass can grow up to 5 feet (1.5 m) wide. It has a stunning green leaf with a wide white stripe. It illuminates the whole area and is an instant eye-catcher in the garden.

**Arundo donax** 'Variegata'

# dry conditions

Analyzing a garden's microclimate is an essential part of picking the most appropriate grass.

**Miscanthus sinensis** 'Puenktchen' tolerates dry and moist conditions

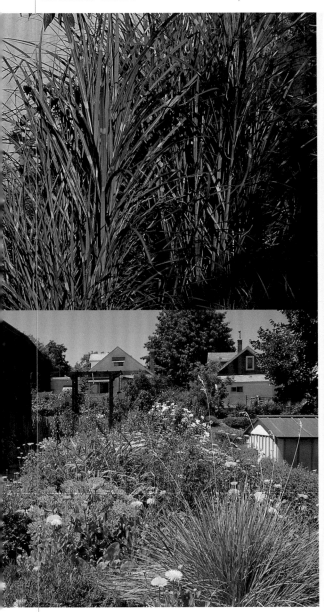

Six or seven centuries ago, repeated droughts forced First Nations peoples to abandon entire areas of the Southwest in North America. In the last century, a tragic drought in the 1930s turned vast areas of the Prairies and Great Plains into dust bowls. Major droughts still occur roughly every 22 years in North America.

A drought is not the same as a dry climate. Drought is a condition that is temporary, although it may last for years. Most gardeners have to contend with partial droughts, or dry spells, brought on by 14 or more days without enough rain.

Ornamental grass gardeners in dry climates can choose from a good selection of plants. In more temperate climates many grasses easily weather dry spells that can devastate other perennials and annuals.

**Helictotrichon sempervirens** (blue oat grass) tolerates drought conditions

**tolerates dry and moist conditions**

*Calamagrostis, Panicum* and *Pennisetum* species grow well in both dry and moist conditions.

**tolerates drought conditions**

*Helictotrichon sempervirens* (blue oat grass) does well in drought as do many of the fine-leafed varieties of *Miscanthus sinensis*, such as 'Gracillimus,' 'Berlin,' 'Morning Light,' and 'Puenktchen.'

Most of the *Festuca* species, including the very popular 'Elijah Blue' and 'Superba,' tolerate drought well.

# dry conditions

**Miscanthus sinensis** 'Berlin'

*Miscanthus sinensis* 'Berlin' tolerates very dry conditions. This newer selection has a spectacular golden flower and can grow to 6 feet (1.8 m). There are five plants in this installation.

*Bouteloua curtipendula* (mosquito grass), a native grass, has a wonderful open structure. In flower it looks like a little cloud of mosquitoes, hence the common name.

**Bouteloua curtipendula** (mosquito grass)

**Pennisetum messiacum** 'Red Bunny Tails'

*Pennisetum messiacum* 'Red Bunny Tails' tolerates dry conditions and flowers in pretty red plumes.

A grouping of *Helictotrichon sempervirens* (blue oat grass).

**Helictotrichon sempervirens** (blue oat grass)

# dry conditions

Variegated **Miscanthus sinensis** 'Puenktchen'

Variegated *Miscanthus sinensis* 'Puenktchen' tolerates dry conditions well.

The fine-leafed *Miscanthus sinensis* 'Morning Light' grows to approximately 4 feet (1.2 m) high and about 3 feet (90 cm) in overall width.

**Miscanthus sinensis** 'Morning Light'

**Sorghastrum nutans**

The magnificent, metallic blue native grass, *Sorghastrum nutans,* growing beside *Rudbeckia* 'Goldsturm.'

*Deschampsia cespitosa* by a water fountain in the Van Dusen Gardens in British Columbia.

**Deschampsia cespitosa**

# shade

Many gardeners, particularly in urban areas, face challenges of gardening in the shade. I am asked more questions about shade-tolerant plants than almost anything else.

People who think of grasses as only sun-loving are pleased to learn that many do not require a sunny site. Grass-like *Carex* species especially do well in shade.

*Calamagrostis arundinacea* var. *brachytricha* in autumn. It flowers late in early September on upright divergent foliage that grows to 30 inches (75 cm) tall and about 2 feet (60 cm) wide. It makes a wonderful cut flower.

**Calamagrostis arundinacea** var. **brachytricha**

**Carex conica** 'Variegata'

*Carex conica* 'Variegata' is the smallest *Carex* we grow. It reaches only 4 to 6 inches (10 to 15 cm) in height and about 6 to 8 inches (15 to 20 cm) in width. The fine-textured blue-green leaves have a white stripe. It works well as a specimen plant in rock gardens or as a ground cover at the feet of *Viburnum lantana*.

*Carex albula* 'Frosty Curls.' A small, fine, mounded plant, it likes moist shade and grows well in containers. The lime green colour harmonizes with and intensifies companion plants like *Heuchera* 'Pewter Veil' (coral bells) with its burgundy and silver leaves.

**Carex albula** 'Frosty Curls'

# shade

**Carex japonica**

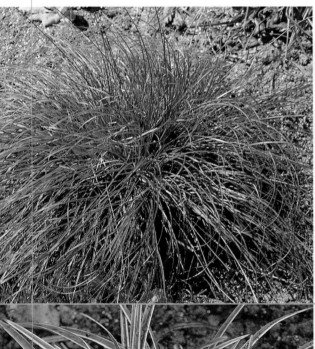

A vigorous, year-old, emerald green *Carex japonica*. In one season it has grown from 6 inches (15 cm) wide in a one-gallon pot to 2 feet (60 cm) inches wide and 10 inches (25 cm) in height. It appears to be quite happy with the half-day of sun and half-day of shade it receives under the *Acer platanoides* 'Crimson King' (red maple) in our front garden. Try planting *C. japonica* with *Persicaria* 'Variegata.'

A young *Carex morrowii* 'Ice Dance.' It's about the same shape and size as its close relative 'Evergold' but 'Ice Dance' has a much thicker leaf and the opposite leaf colour, a white edge on green. It works well as a groundcover with medium-sized *Tiara Hostas*.

**Carex morrowii** 'Ice Dance'

**Carex oshimensis** 'Evergold'

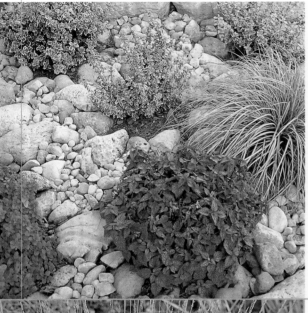

*Carex oshimensis* 'Evergold' in a shady rock garden near Chesley, Ontario. The small mound in the middle right, this grass has a variegated white centre with green-edged leaf. It grows about 1 foot (30 cm) high with an 18-inch (45-cm) spread. Here it is planted with other shade or semi-shade plants, including *Euonymus* in the upper left.

*Molinia caerulea* 'Moorhexe' (purple moor grass). All *Molinia* species grow in shade. 'Moorhexe' is one of the smallest cultivars, growing to about 1 foot (30 cm) in height and 2 feet (60 cm) wide at maturity. It has green foliage and golden-bronze flowers. It adds an open, airy presence to the garden and the foliage turns a lovely yellow in the autumn. Plant it in front of *Miscanthus sinensis*, with *Geranium* 'Ann Folkard' at its feet, for a lovely layered effect.

**Molinia caerulea** 'Moorhexe' (purple moor grass)

# designing with grasses

Pioneer gardener Gertrude Jekyll had a profound understanding of the art of gardening. In *Colour Schemes for the
Flower Garden,* originally published in 1908, a gently dog-
matic Jekyll sharply differentiated between "a collection
of plants" and "a garden," comparing a collection of
plants to a box of paints in wait of a painter.

The following pages address a universe that includes
deserts, scrublands and rock patches of land beside sun-

stealing high-rise buildings, dense woodland, bush, shaded valleys and long cold winters.

Chapter two introduced you to the ornamental grass paint box — an array of temperaments and colours from which to select. As with all gardening, it's important to put the right grass in the right place, taking into consideration specifics like drainage, sunlight and shade, as well as the characteristics, needs and limitations of the plants.

Height, structure, growth habit, texture, colour and seasons of interest are some of the variables.

If plants are the paints in garden composition, then the land — its contours and climate — is the canvas. Creative placement of grasses can impart balance and harmony, provide a stunning focal point or create a sense of unity with large plantings.

The first step in creating a garden is to determine what it will be used for — the intent of the garden. If space is not a problem, it can be divided into quite disparate areas. Perhaps there might be a place for reflection or contemplation, a more open area for children's play and recreation, sheltered areas for dining or special settings for garden sculpture. Other considerations might be interesting pathways for walking, fountains, pools, seating, walls, patios, steps or small structures like trellises. The overall design, or theme, of the garden will determine many of these elements.

There are many schools of thought about garden design, from English cottage to Japanese to Mediterranean. While some approach design from this cultural or historic perspective, others, like us, find the most powerful gardens are those that are designed around the selection of the plants themselves. Whatever the focus, all designs begin by establishing the scale, focal point, perspective and proportion in a planting, using the elementary principles of geometry—line, angle, circle, square and triangle.

Unlike a painting, a garden is a moveable feast of change, which raises the second step in garden design — timing. There is no better group of plants to highlight seasonal glories than grasses. As all-season performers, ornamental grasses adapt to natural land formations in dramatic, bold sweeps. They work equally well delin-eating space, echoing curves and creating screens and borders. Year round, they make superb companions for bulbs, conifers, perennials, shrubs and trees.

Grasses can be used to create exciting new displays, such as a mass planting of a single specimen to create a natural panorama, or to refresh existing beds. Weaving grasses through an established flower bed will give it a new life with texture, colour and punctuation. Ornamental grasses are suited to a wide range of gardens — natural or formal, large or small — they are as suited to the close-up views in the small walled garden of a townhouse as they are to spacious parks with open vistas.

## Four Design Principles

For simplicity, when we select grasses for a design, we use four organizing principles — specimen, scaffold, decorative and natural. Many grasses are versatile enough to fit into more than one of these categories, depending on the setting and the ingenuity of the gardener. The following photographs illustrate how various grasses are used according to these four design principles.

decorative                    natural

# specimens

Like the leading lady in a play, a specimen grass has enough character to do a scene alone in the spotlight. These grasses are focal points.

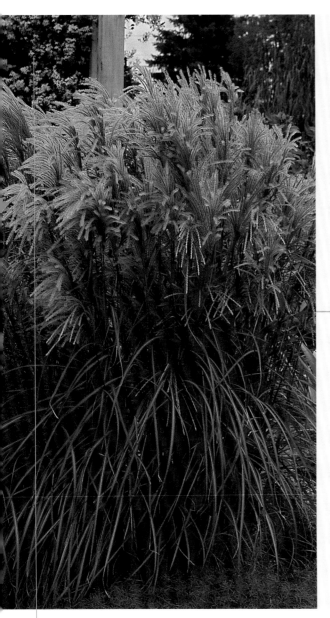

**Miscanthus sinensis** 'Huron Sunrise'

Specimens are selected for unique architectural structure, pleasing foliage or exceptional flower display. They must have enough character to command attention in beds, borders or containers, but they are not necessarily tall. Many medium- and even small-sized grasses perform well in this role.

*Miscanthus sinensis* 'Huron Sunrise' is a fine focal point. It grows to a height of about 4 feet (1.2 m) and flowers early with a rich burgundy flower. It is a wonderful overall performer in dry or moist conditions.

**Pennisetum setaceum** 'Burgundy Giant'

This tender *Pennisetum setaceum* 'Burgundy Giant' (giant purple fountain grass) at Longwood Gardens in Maryland is not hardy in Ontario, where we treat it as an annual. It can grow to about 5 feet (1.5 metres).

*Arundo donax* 'Variegata' (giant variegated reed grass) has white variegated foliage. It is pictured here behind some *Pennisetum alopecuroides* 'Hameln' and a distinctive garden sculpture in Waterloo Gardens, Philadelphia. 'Variegata' thrives in dry or wet conditions and can tower to more than 9 feet (2.7 m) with a girth of 5 feet (1.5 m) in one season.

**Arundo donax** 'Variegata' (giant variegated reed grass)

# specimens

A three-year-old *Miscanthus sinensis* 'Cabaret' (Japanese silver grass) at the Walters Gardens in Zeeland, Michigan. Its 1-inch-wide (2.5-cm) leaves have a cream-white midrib and narrow, dark green margins. It is the boldest of the variegated *M. sinensis* cultivars at a height of about 5 feet (1.5 m) and width of 5 feet (1.5 m). Coupled with fabulous variegated foliage it is a fine focal point.

**Miscanthus sinensis** 'Cabaret' (Japanese silver grass)

**Pennisetum alopecuroides** 'Little Bunny'

One of the miniature contenders in the specimen category is *Pennisetum alopecuroides* 'Little Bunny.' This hardy little member of the fountain grass family has delightful light green foliage and a pale yellow flower in fall. It grows in small clumps and at maturity will be about 8 inches (20 cm) high and 18 inches (45 cm) wide. 'Little Bunny' likes moisture and looks great in a rock garden or near a pond or stream. It is more hardy than its variegated sister 'Little Honey.'

*Calamagrostis* x *acutiflora* 'Karl Foerster,' shown here in a mass planting, also stands alone magnificently. It grows to about 30 inches (75 cm) high and wide and flowers very early. It is spectacular with the blue-flowering *Perovskia atriplicifolia* and *Saccharum ravennae* (hardy pampas grass).

**Calamagrostis** x **acutiflora** 'Karl Foerster'

# scaffolds

Scaffold grasses are the chorus that backs up a diva — the framework that supports and integrates a garden plan.

**Miscanthus sinensis** 'Malepartus'

They form the grid for the garden as a whole and for individual beds. Think of traditional boxwood hedges, which divide a garden into areas for privacy, shelter or atmosphere; in high season they are always eclipsed by showier shrubs and perennials.

When designing with grasses, it is especially important to know what they look like in fall and winter when they are most visible. We favour the hardiest selections with strong outlines that maintain their shape whatever the weather. We select plants with distinctive flower heads that will stay neat or keep their shape throughout the winter. In the top spots in this category are *Miscanthus sinensis* 'Zebrinus,' *Molinia caerulea* ssp. *arundinacea* 'Skyracer' and *Miscanthus sinensis* 'Malepartus.'

**Molinia caerulea** ssp. **arundinacea** 'Skyracer'

*Molinia caerulea* ssp. *arundinacea* 'Skyracer' is the largest plant in this bed of mixed grasses at St. Andrew's Golf Course in Toronto, Ontario.

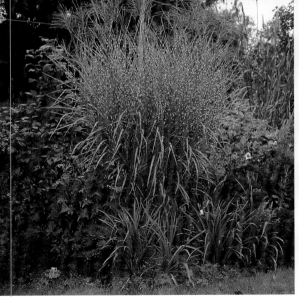

Striped *Miscanthus sinensis* 'Zebrinus' anchors this front yard mixed perennial bed in Strathroy, Ontario.

**Miscanthus sinensis** 'Zebrinus'

# decoratives

The function of grasses in the decorative category is to provide infill or accent for focal points — a supporting, rather than a starring, role. Decoratives dramatize a planting with sound, light and motion.

**Calamagrostis** x **acutiflora** 'Karl Foerster'

*Calamagrostis* x *acutiflora* 'Karl Foerster' poolside in Bala, Ontario. It grows 30 inches (75 cm) high and wide and has a bronze flower in mid- to late summer. It works very well with *Coreopsis* 'Moonbeam' and *Miscanthus sinensis* 'Malepartus.'

The illuminating *Miscanthus sinensis* 'Variegatus' was one of the first grasses we put into a garden setting. A fine specimen plant, it grows to 6 feet (1.8 m) and is pictured here in our production field. Although it is showing a brown flower, 'Variegatus' rarely flowers in Ontario and only where the summers are hottest.

**Miscanthus sinensis** 'Variegatus'

**Panicum virgatum** 'Heavy Metal'

*Panicum virgatum* 'Heavy Metal' has a stunning metallic blue colour that changes to purple in the fall. Unlike some of its relatives, 'Heavy Metal' is very tight and erect in structure. It can grow to a height of about 3 feet (90 cm).

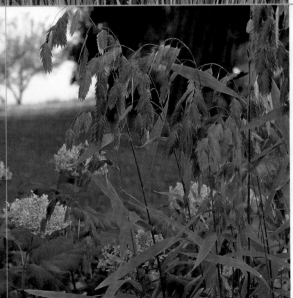

*Chasmanthium latifolium* is noted for both foliage and flower. It is used for erosion control and also in the garden. Its colour progresses from green in summer to copper in autumn, when oat-like flowers bow gracefully from the arching stems.

**Chasmanthium latifolium**

# decoratives

**Panicum virgatum** 'Huron Solstice'

The outstanding copper-leafed *Panicum virgatum* 'Huron Solstice' is a recent introduction. Erect in structure, it grows to 3 feet (90 cm) high and wide.

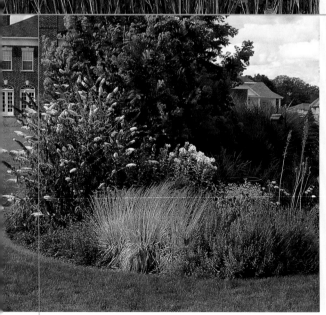

**Molinia caerulea** 'Variegata' (striped purple moor grass)

*Molinia caerulea* 'Variegata' (striped purple moor grass) has cream and green leaves. Depending on the moisture it grows to a height of only 2 to 3 feet (60 to 90 cm). 'Variegata' is slow to mature but it produces superb wheat-coloured flowers on yellow stems that turn purple with pollen as the season moves on. Here it is planted with sweet-scented lavender. In the foreground is a fragrant *Buddleia davidii* (butterfly bush).

**Pennisetum alopecuroides** 'Moudry' (black-flowering pennisetum)

This *Pennisetum alopecuroides* 'Moudry' (black-flowering pennisetum) is about three years old, 30 inches (70 cm) across and 2 feet (60 cm) high. Its spectacular flowers don't appear in the first year or two and don't elongate like 'Rubrum.' A mature plant produces distinctive cascading flowers of deep purple that are radiant in the autumn light.

The best-selling perennial grass for years has been *Helictotrichon sempervirens* (blue oat grass). It is very compact and maintains its striking metallic blue colour into late fall. This versatile plant grows to about 18 inches (45 cm) across and 2 feet (60 cm) tall and tolerates extreme conditions, from dry to wet and sun to shade. Its fine texture complements many different plants. We like to contrast it with the textures of *Artemisia arborescens* 'Powis Castle' and *Heuchera* 'Chocolate Ruffles.'

**Helictotrichon sempervirens** (blue oat grass)

# naturals

The first European settlers in North America described the tall grass prairie as a sea of amber waves. Native grasses — or naturals — are not visitors.

Rooted in North American climate zones, they propagate easily and are extremely hardy, unlike some imported grasses. Native grasses are used in prairie restoration work, for naturalizing and for erosion control. They also have a role to play in garden design.

Native to wet prairies and marshes from Maine to the great plains of North America, the tall variegated *Spartina pectinata* 'Aureomarginata' (prairie cord grass)

**Spartina pectinata** 'Aureomarginata' (prairie cord grass)

### tallest

*Saccharum ravennae* in flower towers to 15 feet (4.6 m). This is a cousin of the majestic native grass *Saccharum giganteum*.

### tall

*Andropogon gerardii* (big bluestem) is sturdy, upright and clump-forming. It can grow to over 6 feet (2 m).

*Sorghastrum nutans* (Indian grass) is one of the most abundant and beautiful tall grasses in the original prairies. It is non-invasive and ideal for naturalizing. Its wonderful bronze flower and metallic blue foliage make it a favourite native grass for the garden as well.

### medium

*Chasmanthium latifolium* (northern sea oats), a deep-rooted grass that can tolerate extremely dry conditions, is being widely used in gardens as well as for erosion control on the eastern seaboard. With a foliage height of 3 to 4 feet (.9 to 1.2 m) and a flower height of 5 to 6 six feet (1.5 to 1.8 m).

*Leymus arenarius glauca* (blue lyme grass), usually found around the edges of lakes and streams in dry, sandy conditions, is very effective for erosion control. Although the flower seeds are edible, it is an invasive spreader. Unless it is in a container, we don't recommend using it in the garden.

# naturals

*Andropogon gerardii* (big bluestem) with a contrasting hardy bamboo. The stems of *A. gerardii* turn blue as summer ends.

**Andropogon gerardii** (big bluestem)

**Bouteloua curtipendula**

In fall, the showy foliage of *Bouteloua curtipendula* turns yellow and its spectacular 2 feet (60-cm) spikelets rise well above the foot-high (30-cm) basal foliage to wave like ribbons in the wind. Remarkably, the flowers temporarily blush back to their summer purple with the first frost.

This variegated *Deschampsia cespitosa* 'Northern Lights' does not like full sun. It grows best in moist conditions and dappled shade.

**Deschampsia cespitosa** 'Northern Lights'. 'Northern Lights' was developed from the native grass *Deschampsia cespitosa*.

# naturals

*Saccharum ravennae* (hardy pampas grass), in flower a magnificent 15-foot (4.6-m) giant, performs well as a single specimen, a decorative or in mass plantings.

**Saccharum ravennae**

**Hordeum jubatum**

Almost every *Hordeum jubatum* (foxtail barley) seed that matures is viable. It is fine in the garden if cut back before seeds mature. It is good for naturalizing and birds love it. *H. jubatum* grows about 18 inches (45 cm) high and about 2 feet (60 cm) wide. Flowers have a purple pink hue and look wonderful as a cut flower before the seeds mature.

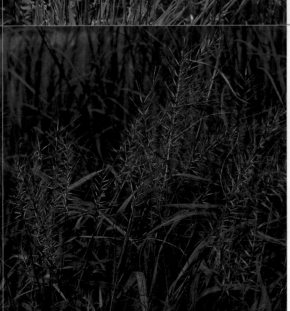

*Hystrix patula* (bottlebrush grass) is named for its flower shape. It grows about 1 to 3 feet (30 to 90 cm) high and about the same in overall width. It is a good border plant for use in natural woodland settings.

**Hystrix patula** (bottlebrush grass)

# naturals

*Sorghastrum nutans* 'Sioux Blue,' a North American native known for its yellow tone in the autumn, is used for naturalizing. It grows in very dry conditions and in all kinds of soil from sandy to heavy clay.

**Sorghastrum nutans** 'Sioux Blue'

**Panicum virgatum**

The open panicles and stunning yellow autumn colour of *Panicum virgatum* make it a great addition to a mixed border garden. *P. virgatum* is native to Ontario.

Medium-sized *Sporobolus heterolepis* (prairie dropseed) wears lovely bronze tones in autumn.

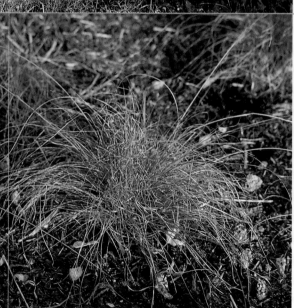

**Sporobolus heterolepis**

# layering

Layering is one of the most exciting challenges when designing with ornamental grasses. It requires planning with an understanding of the plants' growth habits, structures and needs, but most of all, it takes time and experimentation. A good starting point is to consider the size of grasses. The lists below suggests several grasses in the tall, medium and small categories.

By paying close attention to the particulars of shape, leaf structure, flowers, growth habit and seasonal colour within each size category, you will be on your way to becoming a practitioner of the art of layering with ornamental grasses.

# layering

The foliage of the miniature *Miscanthus sinensis* 'Huron Blush' is only about 2 feet (60 cm) high, but when it is in flower the stems and delicate pink panicles tower through and above the foliage to 4 feet (1.2 m). *M. sinensis* 'Grosse Fontäne,' grows to 8 feet (2.4 m) and has a similar flower stretch, but 'Huron Blush' is the only small variety of this species with such a magnificent characteristic. The wide leaves of 'Huron Blush' distinguish it from most other *M. sinensis* cultivars, which are generally very fine-leafed.

**Miscanthus sinensis** 'Huron Blush'

**Small grasses**
**(to 1 foot/ 30 cm)**

*Arrhenatherum elatius* ssp. *bulbosum*
'Variegatus' (bulbous oat grass)

*Carex albula* 'Frosty Curls'
(Frosty Curls hair sedge)

*Carex bergrenii*

*Carex comans* (New Zealand hair sedge)

*Carex conica* 'Variegata'
(miniature variegated sedge)

*Carex morrowii* 'Ice Dance' (Ice Dance sedge)

*Carex morrowii aureo variegata*
(silver variegated Japanese sedge)

*Festuca glauca* 'Boulder Blue' (blue fescue)

*Hakonechloa macra* (hakone grass)

*Holcus mollis* 'Albo-variegatus'
(variegated velvet grass)

*Imperata cylindrica* 'Red Baron'
(Japanese blood grass)

*Koeleria glauca* (large blue hair grass)

**small grasses**

# layering

**medium grasses**
**(1 to 5 feet / 30 cm to 1.5 m)**

*Bouteloua curtipendula* (side oats gramma)

*Calamagrostis arundinacea* var. *brachytricha*
(fall-blooming reed grass)

*Calamagrostis* x *acutiflora* (Karl Foerster)

*Calamagrostis* (Overdam)

*Carex buchananii* (leather leaf sedge)

*Carex elata* 'Bowles' Golden' (yellow sedge)

*Carex muskingumensis* (palm sedge)

*Carex japonica* (Japanese sedge)

*Chasmanthium latifolium* (northern sea oats)

*Deschampsia cespitosa* (tufted hair grass)

*Festuca amethystina* (blue fescue)

*Helictotrichon sempervirens* (blue oat grass)

*Hordeum jubatum* (foxtail barley)

*Hystrix patula* (bottlebrush grass)

*Leymus arenarius* 'Glaucus' (giant dune grass)

*Molinia caerulea* (moor grass)

*Molinia caerulea* 'Variegata' (variegated moor grass)

*Panicum virgatum* (switch grass)

*Pennisetum alopecuroides* (hardy fountain grass)

*Pennisetum alopecuroides* 'Hameln'
(miniature fountain grass)

**medium grasses**

**tall grasses**

**medium grasses (continued)**

*Phalaris arundinacea* (ribbon grass)

*Schizachyrium scoparium* (little bluestem)

*Sporobolus heterolepis* (prairie dropseed)

**tall grasses**
**(6 feet / 1.8 m and over)**

*Arundo donax* (giant reed)

*Spartina pectinata* (prairie cord grass)

*Andropogon gerardii* (big bluestem)

*Molinia caerulea* ssp. *arundinacea* 'Skyracer'
(purple moor grass)

*Miscanthus sinensis* (maiden grass) ✔

*Saccharum ravennae* (hardy pampas grass)

*Sorghastrum nutans* 'Sioux Blue' (Indian grass)

# simple garden plans

These garden plans are meant to encourage you to create your own grass garden
or to mix and match your favourite shrubs and perennials with grasses. Recreate
the plans in your garden or use them as a starting point for your own ideas.

For the most dramatic entry into grass gardening try planting a group with just one variety. Below is a simple group planting of *Panicum virgatum* 'Heavy Metal' around a bench structure at Longwood Gardens in Pennsylvania.

**Panicum virgatum** 'Heavy Metal'

# simple garden plans

This simple and attractive bed contrasts two colourful grasses with a grouping of four upright conifers.

**grasses with upright conifers**

**A** *Juniperus communis* 'Witchita'

**B** *Imperata cylindrica* 'Red Baron'

**C** *Festuca glauca* 'Elijah Blue'.

**Imperata cylindrica** 'Red Baron'

# simple garden plans

This more complex design features a grouping of four spectacular specimens surrounded by a scaffold of 16 grasses and decorated with 14 *Pennisetum alopecuroides* 'Hameln,' and 50 *Helictotrichon sempervirens.*

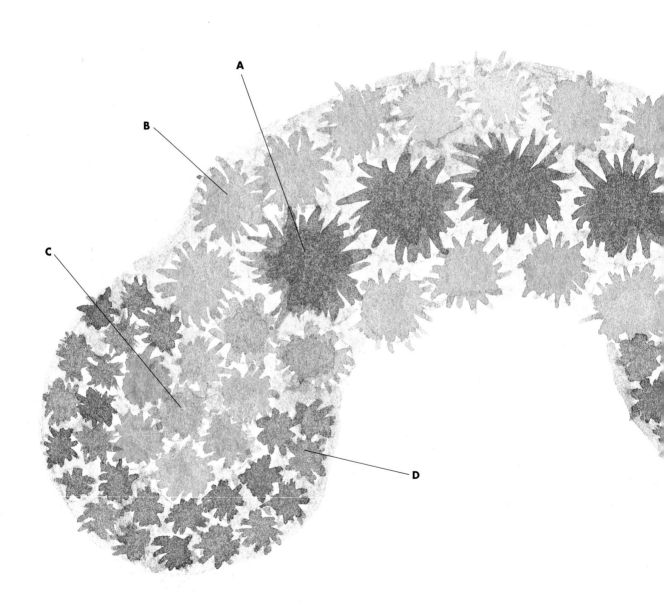

**A** *Molinia caerulea* ssp. *arundinacea* 'Skyracer' (4)

**B** *Panicum virgatum* 'Warrior'(16)

**C** *Pennisetum alopecuroides* 'Hameln' (14)

**D** *Helictotrichon sempervirens* (50)

C

# simple garden plans

My sister Nancy Potter transformed her front yard when she installed four
grasses in an existing perennial bed.

A *Buddleia* 'White Profusion'

B *Miscanthus sinensis* 'Malepartus'

C *Calamagrostis x acutiflora* 'Overdam'

D *Helictotrichon sempervirens*

E *Coreopsis* 'Moonbeam'

F *Pennisetum alopecuroides* 'Hameln'

# simple garden plans

There are eight grasses in this adventuresome, kidney-shaped corner bed designed by enthusiast Jim Dalton in 2002, suggesting how many perennials and shrubs grow well with grasses. Like most avid gardeners, Jim is already making changes.

A  *Prunus 'Newport'*

B  *Cornus alba 'Sibirica Variegata'*

C  *Helictotrichon sempervirens*

D  *Geraniun cantabrigiense 'Biokova'*

E  *Calamagrostis x acutiflora 'Karl Foerster'*

F  *Molinia caerulea ssp. arundinacea
'Skyracer'*

G  *Miscanthus sinensis 'Graziella'*

H  *Deschampsia cespitosa*

I  *Arundo donax*

J  *Sedum 'Autumn Joy'*

K  *Festuca ovina glauca*

L  *Pennisetum alopecuroides 'Hameln'*

# simple garden plans

*Calamagrostis* x *acutiflora* 'Karl Foerster' in a group planting at a Canada/USA border crossing, with water, stone and a bronze sculpture.

**Calamagrostis** x **acutiflora** 'Karl Foerster'

**Miscanthus sinensis** and **Pennisetum alopecuroides**

*Miscanthus sinensis* and *Pennisetum alopecuroides* in a mixed border at the Royal Botanical Gardens in Hamilton, Ontario.

A partly shaded garden with *Calamagrostis arundinacea* var. *brachytricha* and hosta in Bala, Ontario.

**Calamagrostis arundinacea** var. **brachytricha**

# simple garden plans

*Miscanthus sinensis* 'Gracillimus' and *Pennisetum alopecuroides* accenting a garden bench in a small townhouse.

**Miscanthus sinensis** 'Gracillimus' and
**Pennisetum alopecuroides**

**Festuca glauca**

*Festuca glauca* mass planting on a hill at Westridge Farms in Langley, BC.

*Pennisetum alopecuroides* 'Hameln' and the golden hues of *Stipa gigantea* at Kurt Bluemel's pond garden near Baltimore, Maryland.

**Pennisetum alopecuroides** 'Hameln' in foreground

# simple garden plans

**Miscanthus sinensis** 'Variegatus' and **Miscanthus sinensis** 'Strictus'

*Miscanthus sinensis* 'Variegatus' and *Miscanthus sinensis* 'Strictus' in autumn at the Cuddy garden in Strathroy, Ontario.

*Miscanthus sinensis* 'Gracillimus' with evergreens and stone landscaping at an office building in Burlington, Ontario.

**Miscanthus sinensis** 'Gracillimus'

A pink-flowered *Cortaderia selloana* in a Vancouver Island garden.

**Cortaderia selloana** (pink)

# simple garden plans

*Miscanthus sinensis* 'Huron Sunset' in full burgundy flower.

**Miscanthus sinensis** 'Huron Sunset'

*Pennisetum glaucum* (red-leafed millet) a new annual that has great colour and attracts birds.

**Pennisetum glaucum** (red-leafed millet)

# simple garden plans

*Miscanthus sinensis* 'Huron Penetangore' (big dot) is a new introduction with only one or two yellow bands on each leaf.

**Miscanthus sinensis** 'Huron Penetangore'

*Miscanthus sinensis* 'Huron Sunrise,' our first introduction, flowers early with a burgundy flower.

**Miscanthus sinensis** 'Huron Sunrise'

# perennial companions

There are hundreds of perennials that are perfect grass companions — in the sun or shade garden and in all growing and soil conditions. Hostas, ferns and bamboo, however, are especially lovely with hardy ornamental grasses. Evergreen bamboo offers a delightful contrast of colours and textures in the monochromatic winter grass garden. In shade gardens, easy-maintenance ferns and hostas come in a wide range of sizes, shapes, textures and colours.

The following list of favourite grass companions includes botanical and common names, zone hardiness, form, height, flower colour, flowering period and optimal growing conditions. The heights and bloom times are based on Ontario growing conditions.

# perennial companions

| | **Achillea 'Moonshine'** (fern-leafed yarrow) | **Artemisia arborescens 'Powis Castle'** (wormwood) |
|---|---|---|
| **Zone** | 3–8 | 4–9 |
| **Form and height** | Upright; 20" (50 cm) | Upright; 28" (77 cm) |
| **Flower** | Yellow | Silver to yellow or soft green |
| **Bloomtime** | August to September | Not grown for its flower |
| **Growing conditions** | Full sun; drought tolerant | Full sun; drought tolerant |

| | **Anemone 'Honorine Jobert'** (windflower) | **Bambusa 'Fargesia'** (bamboo) |
|---|---|---|
| **Zone** | 4–9 | 5–9 |
| **Form and height** | Upright; 42" (1.5 m) | Upright; 8' (2.5 m) |
| **Flower** | White | — |
| **Bloomtime** | August to September | Rarely flowers |
| **Growing conditions** | Part shade; shade | Full sun to part shade |

| | **Angelica gigas** (Angelica) | **Baptisia australis** (wild indigo) |
|---|---|---|
| **Zone** | 4 | 2–9 |
| **Form and height** | Upright; 42–54" (1.05–1.4 m) | Upright; 3' (90 cm) |
| **Flower** | White | Blue |
| **Bloomtime** | August to September | June to July |
| **Growing conditions** | Full sun | Full sun to part shade; drought tolerant |

### Campanula lactiflora
(bellflower)

| | |
|---|---|
| Zone | 3–7 |
| Form and height | Upright; 28" (75 cm) |
| Flower | Blue |
| Bloomtime | June to July |
| Growing conditions | Full sun to part shade |

### Crambe cordifolia
(sea kale)

| | |
|---|---|
| Zone | 5–9 |
| Form and height | Upright; 5' (1.5 m) |
| Flower | White |
| Bloomtime | April to May |
| Growing conditions | Full sun |

### Cimicifuga racemosa 'Cordifolia' (bugbane)

| | |
|---|---|
| Zone | 3–9 |
| Form and height | Upright; 47" (1.2 m) |
| Flower | White, pink |
| Bloomtime | August to September |
| Growing conditions | Part shade; shade; moisture tolerant |

### Echinacea 'Magnus'
(purple cone flower)

| | |
|---|---|
| Zone | 4–8 |
| Form and height | Upright; 48" (1.2 m) |
| Flower | Purple/red |
| Bloomtime | August to September |
| Growing conditions | Full sun; drought tolerant |

### Coreopsis lanceolata 'Sterntaler' (tickseed)

| | |
|---|---|
| Zone | 4–9 |
| Form and height | Upright; 2' (60 cm) |
| Flower | Yellow |
| Bloomtime | June to September |
| Growing conditions | Full sun |

### Echinops ritro
(globe thistle)

| | |
|---|---|
| Zone | 2–9 |
| Form and height | Upright; 3' (90 cm) |
| Flower | Blue |
| Bloomtime | August to September |
| Growing conditions | Full sun |

## Eupatorium purpureum
(joe pye weed)

| | |
|---|---|
| **Zone** | 5–9 |
| **Form and height** | Upright; 70" (1.78 m) |
| **Flower** | Pink, white, wine |
| **Bloomtime** | August to September |
| **Growing conditions** | Full sun to part shade |

## Geranium phaeum
(cranesbill)

| | |
|---|---|
| **Zone** | 4–9 |
| **Form and height** | Upright; 28" (71 cm) |
| **Flower** | Dark purple |
| **Bloomtime** | June to July |
| **Growing conditions** | Full sun to part shade; moisture and drought tolerant |

## Euphorbia griffithii 'Fireglow'
(spurge)

| | |
|---|---|
| **Zone** | 2–9 |
| **Form and height** | Upright; 28" (71 cm) |
| **Flower** | Orange/red |
| **Bloomtime** | April to May |
| **Growing conditions** | Full sun |

## Helianthus angustifolius
(sunflower)

| | |
|---|---|
| **Zone** | 4–9 |
| **Form and height** | Upright; 7' (2 m) |
| **Flower** | Yellow |
| **Bloomtime** | September to October |
| **Growing conditions** | Full sun; drought tolerant |

## Filipendula rubra 'Venuta Magnifica' (meadowsweet)

| | |
|---|---|
| **Zone** | 2–9 |
| **Form and height** | Upright; 5' (1.5 m) |
| **Flower** | Pink/red |
| **Bloomtime** | August to September |
| **Growing conditions** | Full sun to part shade; moisture tolerant |

## Hemerocallis 'Hyperion'
(daylily)

| | |
|---|---|
| **Zone** | 3–9 |
| **Form and height** | Upright arching; 28" (71 cm) |
| **Flower** | Yellow |
| **Bloomtime** | June to September |
| **Growing conditions** | Full sun to part shade |

## Gaura lindheimeri 'Whirling Butterflies' (butterfly flower)

| | |
|---|---|
| **Zone** | 5–9 |
| **Form and height** | Upright arching; 28" (71 cm) |
| **Flower** | White |
| **Bloomtime** | June to September |
| **Growing conditions** | Full sun to part shade; drought tolerant |

## Heuchera 'Chocolate Ruffles'
(coral bells)

| | |
|---|---|
| **Zone** | 2–9 |
| **Form and height** | Upright; 20" (50 cm) |
| **Flower** | White |
| **Bloomtime** | June to July |
| **Growing conditions** | Full sun to shade |

### Hosta 'Blue Angel'
(plantain lily)

| | |
|---|---|
| **Zone** | 2–9 |
| **Form and height** | Upright arching; 3' (90 cm) |
| **Flower** | White |
| **Bloomtime** | June to July |
| **Growing conditions** | Part shade to shade; moisture tolerant |

### Matteuccia struthiopteris
(ostrich fern)

| | |
|---|---|
| **Zone** | 1–9 |
| **Form and height** | Upright; 30"– 5' (75 cm –1.5 m) |
| **Flower** | Foliage — rich green |
| **Bloomtime** | — |
| **Growing conditions** | Full sun to part shade |

### Iris pallida 'Albo Variegata'
(iris)

| | |
|---|---|
| **Zone** | 4–9 |
| **Form and height** | Upright; 2' (60 cm) |
| **Flower** | Fragrant violet flowers |
| **Bloomtime** | June to July |
| **Growing conditions** | Sun; well drained |

### Monarda 'Gardenview Scarlet'
(bee balm)

| | |
|---|---|
| **Zone** | 3–9 |
| **Form and height** | Upright; 28" (75 cm) |
| **Flower** | Red |
| **Bloomtime** | June to September |
| **Growing conditions** | Full sun to part shade |

### Knautia macedonica
(crimson scabiosa)

| | |
|---|---|
| **Zone** | 5–9 |
| **Form and height** | Upright arching; 2' (60 cm) |
| **Flower** | Deep red |
| **Bloomtime** | June to October |
| **Growing conditions** | Full sun |

### Nepeta mussinii 'Dropmore'
(catmint)

| | |
|---|---|
| **Zone** | 2–9 |
| **Form and height** | Prostrate; 10" (25 cm) |
| **Flower** | Blue |
| **Bloomtime** | June to September |
| **Growing conditions** | Full sun; drought tolerant |

### Ligularia przewalskii
(senecio)

| | |
|---|---|
| **Zone** | 5–9 |
| **Form and height** | Upright; 5' (1.5 m) |
| **Flower** | Yellow spike |
| **Bloomtime** | August to September |
| **Growing conditions** | Part shade to sun; moist |

### Ophiopogon planiscapus
'Ebony Knight' (black mondo grass)

| | |
|---|---|
| **Zone** | 5–9 |
| **Form and height** | Prostrate; 10" (25 cm) |
| **Flower** | Pink flowers/black leaves |
| **Bloomtime** | July to August |
| **Growing conditions** | Full sun to part shade |

## Penstemon digitalis 'Husker Red' (beardtongue)

| | |
|---|---|
| **Zone** | 5–7 |
| **Form and height** | Upright; 28" (75 cm) |
| **Flower** | White |
| **Bloomtime** | June to July |
| **Growing conditions** | Full sun; drought tolerant |

## Perovskia atriplicifolia (russian sage)

| | |
|---|---|
| **Zone** | 5–8 |
| **Form and height** | Upright arching; 39" (1 m) |
| **Flower** | Blue |
| **Bloomtime** | August to October |
| **Growing conditions** | Full sun; drought tolerant |

## Persicaria microcephala 'Red Dragon' (fleece flower)

| | |
|---|---|
| **Zone** | 3–9 |
| **Form and height** | Upright; 20" (50 cm) |
| **Flower** | Pink, white |
| **Bloomtime** | June to July |
| **Growing conditions** | Full sun to shade; drought tolerant |

## Phlox paniculata (summer phlox)

| | |
|---|---|
| **Zone** | 3–9 |
| **Form and height** | Upright; 5' (1.5 m) |
| **Flower** | White |
| **Bloomtime** | July to August |
| **Growing conditions** | Full sun to part shade |

## Rodgersia aesculifolia (Rodger's flower)

| | |
|---|---|
| **Zone** | 5–7 |
| **Form and height** | Upright arching; 38" (90 cm) |
| **Flower** | White |
| **Bloomtime** | June to July |
| **Growing conditions** | Part shade to shade; moisture tolerant |

## Rudbeckia fulgida 'Goldsturm' (black-eyed susan)

| | |
|---|---|
| **Zone** | 3–8 |
| **Form and height** | Upright; 20" (60 cm) |
| **Flower** | Yellow |
| **Bloomtime** | August to September |
| **Growing conditions** | Full sun; drought tolerant |

## Salvia 'Mainacht' (meadow sage)

| | |
|---|---|
| **Zone** | 4–7 |
| **Form and height** | Upright; 1' (30 cm) |
| **Flower** | Purple |
| **Bloomtime** | June to July |
| **Growing conditions** | Full sun; drought tolerant |

## Scabiosa columbaria 'Butterfly Blue' (pincushion flower)

| | |
|---|---|
| **Zone** | 3–8 |
| **Form and height** | Upright arching; 16" (40 cm) |
| **Flower** | Blue |
| **Bloomtime** | June to September |
| **Growing conditions** | Full sun; drought tolerant |

**Sedum 'Autumn Joy'**
(stonecrop)

| | |
|---|---|
| Zone | 2–9 |
| Form and height | Upright; 2' (60 cm) |
| Flower | Red |
| Bloomtime | August to September |
| Growing conditions | Full sun; drought tolerant |

**Stachys 'Helene von Stein'**
(lamb's ear)

| | |
|---|---|
| Zone | 4–8 |
| Form and height | Prostate; 8"–10" (20–25 cm) |
| Flower | Lavender |
| Bloomtime | Rarely flowers |
| Growing conditions | Full sun; drought tolerant |

**Thalictrum flavum 'Glaucum'**
(meadow rue)

| | |
|---|---|
| Zone | 5–9 |
| Form and height | Upright; 5' (1.5 m) |
| Flower | Yellow |
| Bloomtime | July to August |
| Growing conditions | Part shade; moisture tolerant |

**Verbascum chaixii 'Album'**
(mullein)

| | |
|---|---|
| Zone | 4–9 |
| Form and height | Upright; 39" (1 m) |
| Flower | White |
| Bloomtime | June to July |
| Growing conditions | Full sun; drought tolerant |

**Veronica longifolia 'Blue Spires'** (speedwell)

| | |
|---|---|
| Zone | 3–8 |
| Form and height | Upright; 1'–18" (30–45 cm) |
| Flower | Blue, rose |
| Bloomtime | June to July |
| Growing conditions | Full sun; drought tolerant |

**Veronicastrum virginicum**
(culver's root)

| | |
|---|---|
| Zone | 3–9 |
| Form and height | Upright; 5' (1.5 m) |
| Flower | White, pink |
| Bloomtime | June to July |
| Growing conditions | Full sun to part shade |

# grasses at a glance

Use this summary to check the basic characteristics you are interested in. Some of these grasses may not be readily available, but they are all in cultivation. Ask for them at your local nurseries and they may be able to order them for you. As grasses become better known as fine ornamentals, availability will increase.

**Note:** In the following listings, where foliage and flowers are very similar, flower height is not mentioned. Where flowers are significantly taller than foliage, the flower height is noted (the flower height is the total height of the plant when in flower). The size is based on average mature growth in average conditions, but these figures can vary based on conditions such as moisture and sun exposure.

# grasses at a glance

**Acorus gramineus 'Argenteostriatus'**
(sweet flag)

| | |
|---|---|
| **Pronunciation** | ah-KOR-us gra-MIN-ee-us |
| **Zone** | 5–9 |
| **Form** | Small, upright erect |
| **Size** | Foliage 10" (25 cm) Width 1' (30 cm) |
| **Finest seasonal colour** | Summer white and green variegated |
| **Flower colour & timing** | Rarely flowers |
| **Growing conditions** | Sun to shade; ordinary garden conditions to moist |
| **Landscape use** | Single, mass planting, groundcover |
| **Growth habit** | Clumping |

**Alopecurus pratensis 'Aureus'**
(yellow foxtail grass)

| | |
|---|---|
| **Pronunciation** | al-o-PEK-u-rus prah-TEN-sis AW-ree-us |
| **Zone** | 5–9 |
| **Form** | Medium, tufted |
| **Size** | Foliage 6" (15 cm) Flower 18" (45 cm) Width 18" (45 cm) |
| **Finest seasonal colour** | Spring to summer yellow and green variegated |
| **Flower colour & timing** | Yellowish white, spring |
| **Growing conditions** | Sun; ordinary garden conditions to dry |
| **Landscape use** | Single, mass planting, groundcover |
| **Growth habit** | Clumping |

## Andropogon gerardii
(big bluestem)

| | |
|---|---|
| **Pronunciation** | an-droh-POH-gon jer-AR-dee-eye |
| **Zone** | 3–9 |
| **Form** | Tall, upright divergent |
| **Size** | Foliage 14" (36 cm) Flower 5' (1.5 m) Width 3' (90 cm) |
| **Finest seasonal colour** | Spring bright blue green Autumn copper bronze |
| **Flower colour & timing** | Purplish, August–September |
| **Growing conditions** | Sun; ordinary garden conditions to dry |
| **Landscape use** | Single, naturalizing, specimen |
| **Growth habit** | Clumping |

## Arrhenatherum elatius ssp. bulbosum 'Variegatus' (bulbous oat grass)

| | |
|---|---|
| **Pronunciation** | ah-ren-AH-ther-um el-AH-tee-us bul-BOH-sum var-ee-uh-GAH-tus |
| **Zone** | 4–8 |
| **Form** | Mounded |
| **Size** | Foliage 10" (25 cm) Flower 18" (45 cm) Width 1' (30 cm) |
| **Finest seasonal colour** | Spring to summer white variegated |
| **Flower colour & timing** | Flowers white when produced in early summer |
| **Growing conditions** | Partial shade; ordinary garden conditions |
| **Landscape use** | Single, containers, mass planting, groundcover |
| **Growth habit** | Moderately invasive |

# grasses at a glance

## Arundo donax
(giant reed)

| | |
|---|---|
| **Pronunciation** | ah-RUN-doh DOH-nax |
| **Zone** | 5–10, much of Zone 4 in milder winters |
| **Form** | Tall, upright arching |
| **Size** | Foliage 14' (4.3 m) Leaves 3" (7.5 cm) wide Flower 15' (4.6 m) Width 6' (1.8 m) |
| **Finest seasonal colour** | Spring to summer blue-green |
| **Flower colour & timing** | Rarely flowers, except in extremely mild climates |
| **Growing conditions** | Sun; ordinary garden conditions to moist |
| **Landscape use** | Single, screen, specimen |
| **Growth habit** | Moderately invasive |

## Arundo donax 'Variegata'
(striped giant reed)

| | |
|---|---|
| **Pronunciation** | ah-RUN-doh DOH-nax var-ee-uh-GAH-tah |
| **Zone** | 5–10, much of Zone 5 in milder winters |
| **Form** | Tall, upright arching |
| **Size** | Foliage 9' (2.7 m) Leaves 3" (7.5 cm) wide; Flower 10' (3 m) Width 5' (1.5 m) |
| **Finest seasonal colour** | Spring to summer white variegated |
| **Flower colour & timing** | Rarely flowers |
| **Growing conditions** | Sun; ordinary garden conditions to moist |
| **Landscape use** | Single, containers, mosaic, specimen |
| **Growth habit** | Moderately invasive |

## Bouteloua curtipendula
(side oats gramma)

| | |
|---|---|
| **Pronunciation** | boo-tuh-LOO-ah kur-tih-PEN-dyoo-la |
| **Zone** | 4–9 |
| **Form** | Medium, mounded |
| **Size** | **Foliage** 1' (30 cm) **Flower** 2' (60 cm) **Width** 2' (60 cm) |
| **Finest seasonal colour** | **Autumn** yellow |
| **Flower colour & timing** | Purplish, June |
| **Growing conditions** | Sun; ordinary garden conditions to dry |
| **Landscape use** | Single, naturalizing, mass planting |
| **Growth habit** | Clumping |

## Briza media
(quaking grass)

| | |
|---|---|
| **Pronunciation** | BREYE-zah MEE-dee-ah |
| **Zone** | 4–10 |
| **Form** | Small, mounded |
| **Size** | **Foliage** 1' (30 cm) **Flower** 18" (45 cm) **Width** 18" (45 cm) |
| **Finest seasonal colour** | **Spring to summer** green |
| **Flower colour & timing** | Green iridescent turning golden, spring |
| **Growing conditions** | Sun; ordinary garden conditions |
| **Landscape use** | Single, mass planting |
| **Growth habit** | Clumping |

# grasses at a glance

**Bromus inermis 'Skinner's Gold'**
(smooth brome)

| | |
|---|---|
| **Pronunciation** | BRO-mus in-ER-mus |
| **Zone** | 3–9 |
| **Form** | Medium, arching |
| **Size** | **Foliage** 18" (45 cm) **Flower** 2' (60 cm) **Width** 30" (76 cm) |
| **Finest seasonal colour** | **Summer** yellow and green variegated |
| **Flower colour & timing** | Golden bronze, summer |
| **Growing conditions** | Sun; ordinary garden conditions |
| **Landscape use** | Single, mass planting, container |
| **Growth habit** | Invasive |

**Calamagrostis arundinacea** var. **brachytricha**
(fall-blooming reed grass)

| | |
|---|---|
| **Pronunciation** | kal-ah-mah-GROS-tis ah-run-din-AH-see-ah BRAK-ee-trik-ah |
| **Zone** | 5–9 |
| **Form** | Medium, upright divergent |
| **Size** | **Foliage** 20" (51 cm) **Flower** 3' (90 cm) **Width** 30" (76 cm) |
| **Finest seasonal colour** | **Autumn** yellow |
| **Flower colour & timing** | Pinkish turning bronze, late summer |
| **Growing conditions** | Sun to shade; ordinary garden conditions |
| **Landscape use** | Single, mass planting, flower arrangements |
| **Growth habit** | Clumping |

## Calamagrostis × acutiflora 'Karl Foerster'
(feather reed grass)

| | |
|---|---|
| **Pronunciation** | kal-ah-mah-GROS-tis ah-KYOO-tih-flor-ah |
| **Zone** | 4–9 |
| **Form** | Medium, upright divergent |
| **Size** | **Foliage** 30" (75 cm) **Flower** 4' (1.2 m) **Width** 30" (75 cm) |
| **Finest seasonal colour** | **Spring to summer** green foliage with purple flower in summer |
| **Flower colour & timing** | Pinkish turning bronze, summer |
| **Growing conditions** | Sun; ordinary garden conditions |
| **Landscape use** | Single, mass planting, flower arrangements, screen |
| **Growth habit** | Clumping |

## Calamagrostis × acutiflora 'Overdam'
(feather reed grass)

| | |
|---|---|
| **Pronunciation** | kal-ah-mah-GROS-tis ah-KYOO-tih-flor-ah |
| **Zone** | 4–9 |
| **Form** | Medium, upright divergent |
| **Size** | **Foliage** 30" (76 cm) **Flower** 4' (1.2 m) **Width** 30" (76 cm) |
| **Finest seasonal colour** | **Spring to summer** white variegated |
| **Flower colour & timing** | Pinkish turning bronze, summer |
| **Growing conditions** | Sun; ordinary garden conditions |
| **Landscape use** | Single, mass planting, flower arrangements, screen |
| **Growth habit** | Clumping |

# grasses at a glance

**Carex albula 'Frosty Curls'**
(hair sedge)

| | |
|---|---|
| **Pronunciation** | KAIR-ex  ahl-BYOO-lay |
| **Zone** | 5–9 |
| **Form** | Small, mounded |
| **Size** | Foliage 1' (30 cm) Width 14" (36 cm) |
| **Finest seasonal colour** | Summer lime green |
| **Flower colour & timing** | Inconspicuous flowers, June through August |
| **Growing conditions** | Sun to shade; ordinary garden conditions |
| **Landscape use** | Single, mass planting |
| **Growth habit** | Clumping |

**Carex bergrenii**
(bergrenii carex)

| | |
|---|---|
| **Pronunciation** | KAIR-ex BER-gre-NE-eye |
| **Zone** | 5–9 |
| **Form** | Small, mounded |
| **Size** | Foliage 4" (10 cm) Width 14" (36 cm) |
| **Finest seasonal colour** | Summer bronze |
| **Flower colour & timing** | Inconspicuous flowers, June through August |
| **Growing conditions** | Sun to shade; ordinary garden conditions to moist |
| **Landscape use** | Single, mass planting |
| **Growth habit** | Moderately invasive |

## Carex buchananii
(leather leaf sedge)

| | |
|---|---|
| **Pronunciation** | KAIR-ex byoo-kah-NAN-ee-eye |
| **Zone** | 5–9 |
| **Form** | Small, upright divergent |
| **Size** | **Foliage** 2' (60 cm) **Width** 14" (36 cm) |
| **Finest seasonal colour** | **Summer** bronze |
| **Flower colour & timing** | Inconspicuous flowers, June through August |
| **Growing conditions** | Sun to shade; ordinary garden conditions to moist |
| **Landscape use** | Single, mass planting, mosaic |
| **Growth habit** | Clumping |

## Carex buchananii 'Viridis'
(leather leaf sedge)

| | |
|---|---|
| **Pronunciation** | KAIR-ex byoo-kah-NAN-ee-eye |
| **Zone** | 5–9 |
| **Form** | Small, upright divergent |
| **Size** | **Foliage** 2' (60 cm) **Width** 14" (36 cm) |
| **Finest seasonal colour** | **Summer** lime green |
| **Flower colour & timing** | Inconspicuous flowers, June through August |
| **Growing conditions** | Sun to shade; ordinary garden conditions to moist |
| **Landscape use** | Single, mass planting, mosaic |
| **Growth habit** | Clumping |

# grasses at a glance

**Carex caryophyllea 'The Beatles'**
(the Beatles)

| | |
|---|---|
| **Pronunciation** | KAIR-ex cari-o-FEEL-ee-ah |
| **Zone** | 5–9 |
| **Form** | Small, mounded |
| **Size** | **Foliage** 1' (30 cm) **Width** 14" (36 cm) |
| **Finest seasonal colour** | **Summer** green |
| **Flower colour & timing** | Inconspicuous flowers, June through August |
| **Growing conditions** | Sun to shade; ordinary garden conditions |
| **Landscape use** | Single, mass planting |
| **Growth habit** | Clumping |

**Carex comans**
(New Zealand hair sedge)

| | |
|---|---|
| **Pronunciation** | KAIR-ex KOH-manz |
| **Zone** | 5–9 |
| **Form** | Small, mounded |
| **Size** | **Foliage** 1' (30 cm) **Width** 14" (36 cm) |
| **Finest seasonal colour** | **Summer** bronze |
| **Flower colour & timing** | Inconspicuous flowers, June through August |
| **Growing conditions** | Sun to shade; ordinary garden conditions |
| **Landscape use** | Single, mass planting |
| **Growth habit** | Clumping |

## Carex conica 'Variegata'
(miniature variegated sedge)

| | |
|---|---|
| **Pronunciation** | KAIR-ex KON-ih-kah var-ee-uh-GAH-tah |
| **Zone** | 5–9 |
| **Form** | Small, mounded |
| **Size** | Foliage 6" (15 cm) Width 8" (20 cm) |
| **Finest seasonal colour** | Spring to summer silvery white variegation |
| **Flower colour & timing** | Inconspicuous flowers, June through August |
| **Growing conditions** | Sun to shade; ordinary garden conditions |
| **Landscape use** | Single, groundcover, mass planting |
| **Growth habit** | Clumping |

## Carex dolichostachya 'Kaga Nishiki'
(golden fountains)

| | |
|---|---|
| **Pronunciation** | KAIR-ex |
| **Zone** | 5–9 |
| **Form** | Small, mounded |
| **Size** | Foliage 1' (30 cm) Width 14" (36 cm) |
| **Finest seasonal colour** | Spring to summer yellow variegated |
| **Flower colour & timing** | Inconspicuous flowers, June through August |
| **Growing conditions** | Shade to sun; ordinary garden conditions |
| **Landscape use** | Single, mass planting, mosaic, groundcover |
| **Growth habit** | Clumping |

# grasses at a glance

**Carex elata 'Bowles' Golden'**
(yellow sedge)

| | |
|---|---|
| **Pronunciation** | KAIR-ex eh-LAH-tah |
| **Zone** | 5–9 |
| **Form** | Small, arching |
| **Size** | **Foliage** 18" (45 cm) **Width** 14" (36 cm) |
| **Finest seasonal colour** | **Spring to summer** yellow |
| **Flower colour & timing** | Brownish, June–July |
| **Growing conditions** | Shade; ordinary garden conditions to moist |
| **Landscape use** | Single, mosaic, mass planting |
| **Growth habit** | Clumping |

**Carex flacca (glaucus)**
(blue sedge)

| | |
|---|---|
| **Pronunciation** | KAIR-ex FLAH-kah |
| **Zone** | 5–9 |
| **Form** | Small, mounded |
| **Size** | **Foliage** 1' (30 cm) **Width** 2' (60 cm) |
| **Finest seasonal colour** | **Spring to summer** blue-green |
| **Flower colour & timing** | Inconspicuous flowers, June through August |
| **Growing conditions** | Shade to sun; ordinary garden conditions |
| **Landscape use** | Single, mass planting, mosaic, groundcover |
| **Growth habit** | Invasive |

## Carex japonica
(Japanese sedge)

| | |
|---|---|
| **Pronunciation** | KAIR-ex jap-ON-ik-a |
| **Zone** | 5–9 |
| **Form** | Small, mounded |
| **Size** | **Foliage** 10" (25 cm) **Width** 2' (60 cm) |
| **Finest seasonal colour** | **Spring to summer** green |
| **Flower colour & timing** | Blackish, June |
| **Growing conditions** | Shade to sun; ordinary garden conditions |
| **Landscape use** | Single, mass planting, groundcover |
| **Growth habit** | Clumping |

## Carex morrowii 'Fishers Form'
(Fishers carex)

| | |
|---|---|
| **Pronunciation** | KAIR-ex |
| **Zone** | 5–9 |
| **Form** | Small, mounded |
| **Size** | **Foliage** 1' (30 cm) **Width** 14" (36 cm) |
| **Finest seasonal colour** | **Spring to summer** yellow variegated |
| **Flower colour & timing** | Inconspicuous flowers, June through August |
| **Growing conditions** | Shade to sun; ordinary garden conditions |
| **Landscape use** | Single, mass planting, mosaic, groundcover |
| **Growth habit** | Clumping |

# grasses at a glance

**Carex morrowii 'Ice Dance'**
(ice dance sedge)

| | |
|---|---|
| **Pronunciation** | KAIR-ex  mor-ROH-ee-eye |
| **Zone** | 5–9 |
| **Form** | Small, mounded |
| **Size** | Foliage 1' (30 cm) Width 14" (36 cm) |
| **Finest seasonal colour** | Spring to summer white variegated |
| **Flower colour & timing** | Inconspicuous flowers, June through August |
| **Growing conditions** | Shade to sun; ordinary garden conditions |
| **Landscape use** | Single, mass planting, mosaic, groundcover |
| **Growth habit** | Moderately invasive |

**Carex oshimensis 'Evergold'**
(silver variegated Japanese sedge)

| | |
|---|---|
| **Pronunciation** | KAIR-ex osh-ee-MEN-sis |
| **Zone** | 5–9 |
| **Form** | Small, mounded |
| **Size** | Foliage 1' (30 cm) Width 14" (36 cm) |
| **Finest seasonal colour** | Spring to summer yellow variegated |
| **Flower colour & timing** | Inconspicuous flowers, June through August |
| **Growing conditions** | Shade to sun; ordinary garden conditions |
| **Landscape use** | Single, mass planting, mosaic, groundcover |
| **Growth habit** | Clumping |

## Carex muskingumensis
(palm sedge)

| | |
|---|---|
| **Pronunciation** | KAIR-ex mus-kin-goo-MEN-sis |
| **Zone** | 4–9 |
| **Form** | Medium, upright arching |
| **Size** | **Foliage** 2' (60 cm) **Width** 35" (89 cm) |
| **Finest seasonal colour** | **Spring to summer** green |
| **Flower colour & timing** | Greenish, May–June |
| **Growing conditions** | Sun to shade; ordinary garden conditions to moist |
| **Landscape use** | Single, mass planting, groundcover, naturalizing |
| **Growth habit** | Moderately invasive |

## Carex pendula
(fringe sedge)

| | |
|---|---|
| **Pronunciation** | KAIR-ex PEN-dyoo-lah |
| **Zone** | 5–9 |
| **Form** | Medium, upright arching |
| **Size** | **Foliage** 4' (1.2 m) **Flower** 5' (1.5 m) **Width** 4' (1.2 m) |
| **Finest seasonal colour** | **Spring to summer** green |
| **Flower colour & timing** | Brownish, July–August |
| **Growing conditions** | Sun to shade; ordinary garden conditions to moist |
| **Landscape use** | Single, mass planting, groundcover, naturalizing |
| **Growth habit** | Clumping |

# grasses at a glance

**Carex plantaginea**
(plantain leafed sedge)

| | |
|---|---|
| **Pronunciation** | KAIR-ex plan-ta-jin-EE-ah |
| **Zone** | 4–9 |
| **Form** | Small, mounding |
| **Size** | **Foliage** 1' (30 cm) **Width** 1' (30 cm) |
| **Finest seasonal colour** | **Summer** green |
| **Flower colour & timing** | Inconspicuous flowers, April–May |
| **Growing conditions** | Shade; ordinary garden conditions to dry |
| **Landscape use** | Single, mass planting, groundcover, naturalizing |
| **Growth habit** | Clumping |

**Carex siderosticha 'Island Brocade'**
(creeping golden variegated broad-leafed sedge)

| | |
|---|---|
| **Pronunciation** | KAIR-ex sih-der-OH-stih-kah |
| **Zone** | 5–9 |
| **Form** | Small, mounding |
| **Size** | **Foliage** 1' (30 cm) **Width** 1' (30 cm) |
| **Finest seasonal colour** | **Summer** green and gold variegated |
| **Flower colour & timing** | Inconspicuous flowers, June through August |
| **Growing conditions** | Shade; ordinary garden conditions to moist |
| **Landscape use** | Single, mass planting, groundcover, naturalizing |
| **Growth habit** | Moderately invasive |

### Carex siderosticha 'Variegata'
(creeping variegated broad-leafed sedge)

| | |
|---|---|
| **Pronunciation** | KAIR-ex sih-der-OH-stih-kah var-ee-uh-GAH-tah |
| **Zone** | 5–9 |
| **Form** | Small, mounding |
| **Size** | **Foliage** 1' (30 cm) **Width** 1' (30 cm) |
| **Finest seasonal colour** | **Summer** green and white variegated |
| **Flower colour & timing** | Brownish black, June–July |
| **Growing conditions** | Shade; ordinary garden conditions to moist |
| **Landscape use** | Single, mass planting, groundcover, naturalizing |
| **Growth habit** | Moderately invasive |

### Chasmanthium latifolium
(northern sea oats)

| | |
|---|---|
| **Pronunciation** | kas-MAN-thee-um lat-ih-FOL-ee-um |
| **Zone** | 5–9 |
| **Form** | Medium, upright arching |
| **Size** | **Foliage** 35" (89 cm) **Flower** 4' (1.2 m) **Width** 2' (60 cm) |
| **Finest seasonal colour** | **Autumn** bright yellow |
| **Flower colour & timing** | Green turning copper, June–September–winter |
| **Growing conditions** | Sun to shade; ordinary garden conditions to dry |
| **Landscape use** | Single, naturalizing, flower arrangements, mass planting |
| **Growth habit** | Clumping |

# grasses at a glance

## Cortaderia selloana
(pampas grass)

| | |
|---|---|
| **Pronunciation** | kor-tah-DEER-ee-ah sell-oh-AN-ah |
| **Zone** | 8–10 |
| **Form** | Tall, upright arching |
| **Size** | Foliage 5' (1.5 m) Flower 8' (2.5 m) Width 5' (1.5 m) |
| **Finest seasonal colour** | Late summer green |
| **Flower colour & timing** | Pink or white; August–September–winter |
| **Growing conditions** | Sun; ordinary garden conditions |
| **Landscape use** | Single, mass planting |
| **Growth habit** | Clumping |

## Deschampsia cespitosa
(tufted hair grass)

| | |
|---|---|
| **Pronunciation** | deh-SHAMP-see-ah ses-pih-TOH-sah |
| **Zone** | 3–8 |
| **Form** | Medium, mounded |
| **Size** | Foliage 16" (40 cm) Flower 42" (106 cm) Width 35" (89 cm) |
| **Finest seasonal colour** | Summer green |
| **Flower colour & timing** | Yellow to gold, May–June |
| **Growing conditions** | Sun to shade; ordinary garden conditions |
| **Landscape use** | Single, mass planting |
| **Growth habit** | Clumping |

**Deschampsia cespitosa 'Northern Lights'**
(variegated tufted hair grass)

| | |
|---|---|
| **Pronunciation** | deh-SHAMP-see-ah ses-pih-TOH-sah |
| **Zone** | 4–8 |
| **Form** | Small, mounded |
| **Size** | **Foliage** 10" (25 cm) **Width** 14" (36 cm) |
| **Finest seasonal colour** | **Summer** white and green variegated |
| **Flower colour & timing** | Yellow to gold, May–June |
| **Growing conditions** | Sun to shade; ordinary garden conditions |
| **Landscape use** | Single, mass planting |
| **Growth habit** | Clumping |

**Eragrostis trichodes**
(love grass)

| | |
|---|---|
| **Pronunciation** | air-ah-GROS-tis trih-KOH-deez |
| **Zone** | 5–9 |
| **Form** | Medium, mounded |
| **Size** | **Foliage** 2' (60 cm) **Flower** 3' (90 cm) **Width** 3' (90 cm) |
| **Finest seasonal colour** | **Summer** green |
| **Flower colour & timing** | Amethyst pink, late July |
| **Growing conditions** | Sun; well-drained soil |
| **Landscape use** | Single, mass planting |
| **Growth habit** | Clumping |

# grasses at a glance

**Eriophorum angustifolium**
(cotton grass)

| | |
|---|---|
| **Pronunciation** | air-ee-OH-for-um an-gus-tif-OL-e-um |
| **Zone** | 4–7 |
| **Form** | Medium, arching |
| **Size** | Foliage 1' (30 cm) Flower 2' (60 cm) Width 2' (60 cm) |
| **Finest seasonal colour** | Spring flowers white cottony heads |
| **Flower colour & timing** | White, May |
| **Growing conditions** | Sun; ordinary garden conditions to moist |
| **Landscape use** | Single, mass planting, containers |
| **Growth habit** | Clumping |

**Festuca amethystina 'Superba'**
(rainbow fescue)

| | |
|---|---|
| **Pronunciation** | fes-TOO-kah am-eh-this-TEE-nah |
| **Zone** | 4–8 |
| **Form** | Medium, tufted |
| **Size** | Foliage 1' (30 cm) Flower 2' (60 cm) Width 18" (46 cm) |
| **Finest seasonal colour** | Summer blue foliage with rainbow-coloured stems |
| **Flower colour & timing** | Purplish, May–June |
| **Growing conditions** | Sun; ordinary garden conditions to dry |
| **Landscape use** | Single, mass planting |
| **Growth habit** | Clumping |

**Festuca glauca 'Boulder Blue'**
(blue fescue)

| | |
|---|---|
| **Pronunciation** | fes-TOO-kah GLOU-kah |
| **Zone** | 4–9 |
| **Form** | Small, tufted |
| **Size** | Foliage 1' (30 cm) Flower 14" (36 cm) Width 14" (36 cm) |
| **Finest seasonal colour** | Spring to summer powder blue |
| **Flower colour & timing** | Bluish, May–June |
| **Growing conditions** | Sun; ordinary garden conditions to dry |
| **Landscape use** | Single, mosaic, mass planting |
| **Growth habit** | Clumping |

**Festuca glauca 'Elijah Blue' 'Sea Urchin'**
(sea urchin fescue)

| | |
|---|---|
| **Pronunciation** | fes-TOO-kah GLOU-kah |
| **Zone** | 4–9 |
| **Form** | Small, tufted |
| **Size** | Foliage 1' (30 cm) Flower 14" (36 cm) Width 14" (36 cm) |
| **Finest seasonal colour** | Spring to summer blue |
| **Flower colour & timing** | Bluish, May–June |
| **Growing conditions** | Sun; ordinary garden conditions |
| **Landscape use** | Single, mosaic, mass planting |
| **Growth habit** | Clumping |

# grasses at a glance

**Festuca ovina glauca**
(blue fescue)

| | |
|---|---|
| **Pronunciation** | fes-TOO-kah oh-VEE-nah GLOU-kah |
| **Zone** | 4–9 |
| **Form** | Small, tufted |
| **Size** | **Foliage** 1' (30 cm) **Flower** 18" (45 cm) **Width** 18" (45 cm) |
| **Finest seasonal colour** | **Spring to summer** blue |
| **Flower colour & timing** | Bluish, May–June |
| **Growing conditions** | Sun; ordinary garden conditions |
| **Landscape use** | Single, mosaic, mass planting |
| **Growth habit** | Clumping |

**Glyceria maxima 'Variegata'**
(Variegated manna grass)

| | |
|---|---|
| **Pronunciation** | GLIH-seer-ee-ah MAX-ih-mah var-ee-uh-GAH-tah |
| **Zone** | 5–10 |
| **Form** | Medium, upright arching |
| **Size** | **Foliage** 2' (60 cm) **Flower** 30" (75 cm) **Width** 3' (90 cm) |
| **Finest seasonal colour** | **Summer** white and green variegated |
| **Flower colour & timing** | Seldom flowers |
| **Growing conditions** | Sun; ordinary garden conditions to moist |
| **Landscape use** | Single, groundcover, mosaic, mass planting |
| **Growth habit** | Moderately invasive |

## Hakonechloa macra
(hakone grass)

| | |
|---|---|
| **Pronunciation** | hah-koh-neh-KLOH-ah MAK-rah |
| **Zone** | 5–9 |
| **Form** | Small, mounded |
| **Size** | **Foliage** 1' (30 cm) **Width** 2' (60 cm) |
| **Finest seasonal colour** | **Summer** green **Autumn/Winter** brilliant bronze |
| **Flower colour & timing** | Light bronze, late summer |
| **Growing conditions** | Shade; ordinary garden conditions |
| **Landscape use** | Single, groundcover, mosaic, mass planting |
| **Growth habit** | Clumping |

## Hakonechloa macra 'Aureola'
(golden variegated hakone grass)

| | |
|---|---|
| **Pronunciation** | hah-koh-neh-KLOH-ah MAK-rah aw-ree-OH-la |
| **Zone** | 5–9 |
| **Form** | Small, mounded |
| **Size** | **Foliage** 1' (30 cm) **Width** 2' (60 cm) |
| **Finest seasonal colour** | **Spring to summer** yellow variegated |
| **Flower colour & timing** | Light bronze, late summer |
| **Growing conditions** | Shade; ordinary garden conditions |
| **Landscape use** | Single, groundcover, containers |
| **Growth habit** | Clumping |

# grasses at a glance

**Helictotrichon sempervirens**
(blue oat grass)

| | |
|---|---|
| **Pronunciation** | hel-ik-toh-TREE-kon sem-per-VEYE-renz |
| **Zone** | 4–8 |
| **Form** | Medium, mounded |
| **Size** | Foliage 16" (40 cm) Flower 46" (1.2 m) Width 2' (60 cm) |
| **Finest seasonal colour** | Spring to summer winter blue |
| **Flower colour & timing** | Golden, June |
| **Growing conditions** | Sun to part shade; ordinary garden conditions to dry |
| **Landscape use** | Single, mosaic, mass planting |
| **Growth habit** | Clumping |

**Holcus mollis 'Albo-variegatus'**
(variegated velvet grass)

| | |
|---|---|
| **Pronunciation** | HOL-kus MOL-us AL-bo var-ee-uh-GAH-tus |
| **Zone** | 5–8 |
| **Form** | Small, mounded |
| **Size** | Foliage 6" (15 cm) Width 1' (30 cm) |
| **Finest seasonal colour** | Spring to summer white variegated |
| **Flower colour & timing** | White, June |
| **Growing conditions** | Part shade; ordinary garden conditions |
| **Landscape use** | Single, mosaic, mass planting, groundcover |
| **Growth habit** | Moderately invasive |

## Hordeum jubatum
(foxtail barley)

| | |
|---|---|
| **Pronunciation** | hor-DEE-um joo-BAH-tum |
| **Zone** | 4–7 |
| **Form** | Medium, arching |
| **Size** | **Foliage** 18" (45 cm) **Flower** 2' (60 cm) **Width** 2' (60 cm) |
| **Finest seasonal colour** | **Spring to summer** green |
| **Flower colour & timing** | light purple, June |
| **Growing conditions** | Sun; ordinary garden conditions |
| **Landscape use** | Single, naturalizing, mass planting, flower arrangements |
| **Growth habit** | Clumping |

## Hystrix patula
(bottlebrush grass)

| | |
|---|---|
| **Pronunciation** | HEYE-striks pah-TOO-lah |
| **Zone** | 4–7 |
| **Form** | Medium, arching |
| **Size** | **Foliage** 1' (30 cm) **Flower** 2' (60 cm) **Width** 2' (60 cm) |
| **Finest seasonal colour** | **Summer** green |
| **Flower colour & timing** | Greenish, June |
| **Growing conditions** | Shade; ordinary garden conditions to dry |
| **Landscape use** | Single, naturalizing, flower arrangements, mass planting |
| **Growth habit** | Clumping |

# grasses at a glance

**Imperata cylindrica 'Red Baron'**
(Japanese blood grass)

| | |
|---|---|
| **Pronunciation** | im-per-AH-tah |
| **Zone** | 5–9 |
| **Form** | Small, upright erect |
| **Size** | Foliage 16" (40 cm) Width 18" (45 cm) |
| **Finest seasonal colour** | Spring to summer and autumn blood red |
| **Flower colour & timing** | Does not produce flowers |
| **Growing conditions** | Sun; ordinary garden conditions to moist |
| **Landscape use** | Single, groundcover, containers, mass planting |
| **Growth habit** | Moderately invasive |

**Koeleria glauca**
(large blue hair grass)

| | |
|---|---|
| **Pronunciation** | koh-LAIR-ee-ah GLOU-kah |
| **Zone** | 4–8 |
| **Form** | Small, tufted |
| **Size** | Foliage 1' (30 cm) Width 18" (45 cm) |
| **Finest seasonal colour** | Spring to summer blue |
| **Flower colour & timing** | Blue-green, May–June |
| **Growing conditions** | Sun; ordinary garden conditions |
| **Landscape use** | Single, mass planting, naturalizing |
| **Growth habit** | Clumping |

## Leymus arenarius 'Glauca'
(blue lyme rye)

| | |
|---|---|
| **Pronunciation** | Lee-mus ar-EEN-arus GLOU-kus |
| **Zone** | 4–9 |
| **Form** | Medium, arching |
| **Size** | Foliage 30" (75 cm) Flower 42" (106 cm) Width 2' (60 cm) |
| **Finest seasonal colour** | Spring to summer blue |
| **Flower colour & timing** | Bronze, June–July |
| **Growing conditions** | Sun; ordinary garden conditions to dry |
| **Landscape use** | Single, containers, mass planting, erosion control |
| **Growth habit** | Invasive |

## Luzula nivea
(snowy woodrush)

| | |
|---|---|
| **Pronunciation** | loo-ZOO-lah NIV-ee-ah |
| **Zone** | 4–9 |
| **Form** | Small, tufted |
| **Size** | Foliage 8" (20 cm) Flower 1' (30 cm) Width 1' (30 cm) |
| **Finest seasonal colour** | Spring to summer green |
| **Flower colour & timing** | White flowers, May–June |
| **Growing conditions** | Sun to shade; ordinary garden conditions |
| **Landscape use** | Single, mass planting |
| **Growth habit** | Clumping |

# grasses at a glance

**Luzula sylvatica**
(greater woodrush)

| | |
|---|---|
| **Pronunciation** | loo-ZOO-lah sill-VAH-tee-kah |
| **Zone** | 4–9 |
| **Form** | Small, tufted |
| **Size** | Foliage 8" (20 cm) Flower 1' (30 cm) Width 1' (30 cm) |
| **Finest seasonal colour** | Spring to summer, green leaves |
| **Flower colour & timing** | Yellow green flowers, May–June |
| **Growing conditions** | Sun to shade; ordinary garden conditions |
| **Landscape use** | Single, mass planting |
| **Growth habit** | Clumping |

**Milium effusum 'Aureum'**
(golden wood millet)

| | |
|---|---|
| **Pronunciation** | MIL-ee-um eh-FYOO-sum AW-ree-um |
| **Zone** | 5–9 |
| **Form** | Small, tufted |
| **Size** | Foliage 1' (30 cm) Flower 2' (60 cm) Width 2' (60 cm) |
| **Finest seasonal colour** | Summer yellow |
| **Flower colour & timing** | Golden yellow; May–June |
| **Growing conditions** | Part shade; ordinary garden conditions to moist |
| **Landscape use** | Single, mass planting |
| **Growth habit** | Loosely clumping |

## Miscanthus floridulus
(Siberian bamboo)

| | |
|---|---|
| **Pronunciation** | mis-KAN-thus FLO-rid-UL-us |
| **Zone** | 4–9 |
| **Form** | Tall, upright arching |
| **Size** | **Foliage** 14' (4.2 m) **Flower** 15' (4.6 m) **Width** 6' (2 m) |
| **Finest seasonal colour** | **Autumn** blonde |
| **Flower colour & timing** | Rarely flowers, late November |
| **Growing conditions** | Sun; ordinary garden conditions to moist |
| **Landscape use** | Single, mass planting, screen |
| **Growth habit** | Moderately invasive |

## Miscanthus purpurascens
(flame grass)

| | |
|---|---|
| **Pronunciation** | mis-KAN-thus pur-pur-AH-senz |
| **Zone** | 4–9 |
| **Form** | Tall, upright arching |
| **Size** | **Foliage** 4' (1.2 m) **Flower** 5' (1.5 m) **Width** 3' (90 cm) |
| **Finest seasonal colour** | **Autumn** red |
| **Flower colour & timing** | White, September |
| **Growing conditions** | Sun; ordinary garden conditions |
| **Landscape use** | Single, mosaic, mass planting, flower arrangements |
| **Growth habit** | Clumping |

# grasses at a glance

**Miscanthus sinensis 'Arabesque'**
(maiden grass)

| | |
|---|---|
| **Pronunciation** | mis-KAN-thus sin-EN-sis |
| **Zone** | 4–9 |
| **Form** | Medium, upright arching |
| **Size** | **Foliage** 4' (1.2 m) **Flower** 5' (1.5 m) **Width** 3' (90 cm) |
| **Finest seasonal colour** | **Summer to autumn** blonde |
| **Flower colour & timing** | Pink turning white, September |
| **Growing conditions** | Sun; ordinary garden conditions |
| **Landscape use** | Single, mosaic, mass planting, flower arrangements |
| **Growth habit** | Clumping |

**Miscanthus sinensis 'Berlin'**
(Japanese silver grass)

| | |
|---|---|
| **Pronunciation** | mis-KAN-thus sin-EN-sis |
| **Zone** | 5–9 |
| **Form** | Tall, upright arching |
| **Size** | **Foliage** 6' (1.8 m) **Flower** 7' (2.1 m) **Width** 5' (1.5 m) |
| **Finest seasonal colour** | **Spring to summer** green |
| **Flower colour & timing** | Golden, September |
| **Growing conditions** | Sun; ordinary garden conditions to dry |
| **Landscape use** | Single, mass planting, flower arrangements |
| **Growth habit** | Clumping |

## Miscanthus sinensis 'Cabaret'
(Japanese silver grass)

| | |
|---|---|
| **Pronunciation** | mis-KAN-thus sin-EN-sis |
| **Zone** | 6–9 |
| **Form** | Tall, upright arching |
| **Size** | **Foliage** 5' (1.5 m) **flower** 6' (1.8 m) **width** 5' (1.5 m) |
| **Finest seasonal colour** | **Autumn** white variegated |
| **Flower colour & timing** | Copper, October–November |
| **Growing conditions** | Sun; ordinary garden conditions |
| **Landscape use** | Single, mosaic, mass planting |
| **Growth habit** | Clumping |

## Miscanthus sinensis 'Gracillimus'
(maiden grass)

| | |
|---|---|
| **Pronunciation** | mis-KAN-thus sin-EN-sis gra-SILL-ih-mus |
| **Zone** | 5–9 |
| **Form** | Tall, upright arching |
| **Size** | **Foliage** 5' (1.5 m) **Flower** 6' (1.8 m) **Width** 5' (1.5m) |
| **Finest seasonal colour** | **Winter** blonde |
| **Flower colour & timing** | Copper, November |
| **Growing conditions** | Sun; ordinary garden conditions |
| **Landscape use** | Single, mass planting, flower arrangements |
| **Growth habit** | Clumping |

# grasses at a glance

## Miscanthus sinensis 'Graziella'
(Japanese silver grass)

| | |
|---|---|
| **Pronunciation** | mis-KAN-thus sin-EN-sis |
| **Zone** | 5–9 |
| **Form** | Tall, upright arching |
| **Size** | **Foliage** 5' (1.5 m) **Flower** 6' (1.8 m) **Width** 5' (1.5 m) |
| **Finest seasonal colour** | **Autumn to winter** blonde |
| **Flower colour & timing** | White, September |
| **Growing conditions** | Sun; ordinary garden conditions |
| **Landscape use** | Single, mass planting, flower arrangements |
| **Growth habit** | Clumping |

## Miscanthus sinensis 'Grosse Fontaine'
(large fountain Japanese silver grass)

| | |
|---|---|
| **Pronunciation** | mis-KAN-thus sin-EN-sis |
| **Zone** | 5–9 |
| **Form** | Tall, upright arching |
| **Size** | **Foliage** 6' (1.8 m) **Flower** 8' (2.4 m) **Width** 6' (1.8 m) |
| **Finest seasonal colour** | **Winter** blonde |
| **Flower colour & timing** | Pink, September |
| **Growing conditions** | Sun; ordinary garden conditions |
| **Landscape use** | Single, mass planting, flower arrangements |
| **Growth habit** | Clumping |

**Miscanthus sinensis 'Huron Blush'**
(Huron maiden grass)

| | |
|---|---|
| **Pronunciation** | mis-KAN-thus sin-EN-sis |
| **Zone** | 4–9 |
| **Form** | Medium, upright arching |
| **Size** | **Foliage** 3' (90 cm) **Flower** 4' (1.2 m) **Width** 3' (90 cm) |
| **Finest seasonal colour** | **Summer** green **Winter** blonde |
| **Flower colour & timing** | Blush pink, September |
| **Growing conditions** | Sun; ordinary garden conditions |
| **Landscape use** | Single, mass planting, flower arrangements, mosaic |
| **Growth habit** | Clumping |

**Miscanthus sinensis 'Huron Penetangore'**
(big dot)

| | |
|---|---|
| **Pronunciation** | mis-KAN-thus sin-EN-sis |
| **Zone** | 4–9 |
| **Form** | Tall, upright arching |
| **Size** | **Foliage** 5' (1.5 m) **Flower** 6' (1.8 m) **Width** 5' (1.5 m) |
| **Finest seasonal colour** | **Spring to summer** yellow variegated |
| **Flower colour & timing** | Pink, September–October |
| **Growing conditions** | Sun; ordinary garden conditions |
| **Landscape use** | Single, mass planting, flower arrangements, screen |
| **Growth habit** | Clumping |

# grasses at a glance

**Miscanthus sinensis 'Huron Sentinel'**
(maiden grass)

| | |
|---|---|
| **Pronunciation** | mis-KAN-thus sin-EN-sis |
| **Zone** | 4–9 |
| **Form** | Tall, upright arching |
| **Size** | Foliage 5' (1.5 m) Flower 6' (2 m) Width 5' (1.5 m) |
| **Finest seasonal colour** | Summer green Winter blonde |
| **Flower colour & timing** | Bronze, late September |
| **Growing conditions** | Sun; ordinary garden conditions |
| **Landscape use** | Single, mass planting, flower arrangements, mosaic |
| **Growth habit** | Clumping |

**Miscanthus sinensis 'Huron Sunrise'**
(Huron maiden grass)

| | |
|---|---|
| **Pronunciation** | mis-KAN-thus sin-EN-sis |
| **Zone** | 4–9 |
| **Form** | Tall, upright arching |
| **Size** | Foliage 4' (1.2 m) Flower 5' (1.5 m) Width 4' (1.2 m) |
| **Finest seasonal colour** | Summer green Winter blonde |
| **Flower colour & timing** | Burgundy, August |
| **Growing conditions** | Sun; ordinary garden conditions |
| **Landscape use** | Single, mass planting, flower arrangements, mosaic |
| **Growth habit** | Clumping |

## Miscanthus sinensis 'Huron Sunset'
(maiden grass)

| | |
|---|---|
| **Pronunciation** | mis-KAN-thus sin-EN-sis |
| **Zone** | 4–9 |
| **Form** | Medium, upright arching |
| **Size** | **Foliage** 3' (90 cm) **Flower** 4' (1.2 m) **Width** 3' (90 cm) |
| **Finest seasonal colour** | **Summer** green **Winter** blonde |
| **Flower colour & timing** | Burgundy, August |
| **Growing conditions** | Sun; ordinary garden conditions |
| **Landscape use** | Single, mass planting, flower arrangements, mosaic |
| **Growth habit** | Clumping |

## Miscanthus sinensis 'Little Zebra'
(little zebra grass)

| | |
|---|---|
| **Pronunciation** | mis-KAN-thus sin-EN-sis |
| **Zone** | 4–9 |
| **Form** | Medium, upright arching |
| **Size** | **Foliage** 2' (60 cm) **Flower** 3' (90 cm) **Width** 3' (90 cm) |
| **Finest seasonal colour** | **Autumn** blonde, yellow and green variegated |
| **Flower colour & timing** | Pink, September–October |
| **Growing conditions** | Sun; ordinary garden conditions |
| **Landscape use** | Single, mosaic, mass planting, flower arrangements |
| **Growth habit** | Clumping |

# grasses at a glance

**Miscanthus sinensis 'Malepartus'**
(large fountain Japanese silver grass)

| | |
|---|---|
| **Pronunciation** | mis-KAN-thus sin-EN-sis |
| **Zone** | 4–9 |
| **Form** | Tall, upright arching |
| **Size** | Foliage 6' (1.8 m) Flower 7' (2.1 m) Width 5' (1.5 m) |
| **Finest seasonal colour** | Winter blonde |
| **Flower colour & timing** | Pink, August |
| **Growing conditions** | Sun; ordinary garden conditions |
| **Landscape use** | Single, mass planting, flower arrangements |
| **Growth habit** | Clumping |

**Miscanthus sinensis 'Morning Light'**
(miniature variegated grass)

| | |
|---|---|
| **Pronunciation** | mis-KAN-thus sin-EN-sis |
| **Zone** | 4–9 |
| **Form** | Medium, upright arching |
| **Size** | Foliage 4' (1.2 m) Flower 4' (1.2 m) Width 3' (90 cm) |
| **Finest seasonal colour** | Summer white and green variegated Autumn blonde |
| **Flower colour & timing** | Bronze, November |
| **Growing conditions** | Sun; ordinary garden conditions |
| **Landscape use** | Single, mosaic, mass planting, flower arrangements |
| **Growth habit** | Clumping |

## Miscanthus sinensis 'Puenktchen'
(little dot)

| | |
|---|---|
| **Pronunciation** | mis-KAN-thus sin-EN-sis |
| **Zone** | 4–9 |
| **Form** | Tall, upright arching |
| **Size** | **Foliage** 4' (1.2 m) **Flower** 5' (1.5 m) **Width** 3' (90 cm) |
| **Finest seasonal colour** | **Autumn** blonde, yellow and green variegated |
| **Flower colour & timing** | Pinkish, September–October |
| **Growing conditions** | Sun; ordinary garden conditions |
| **Landscape use** | Single, mosaic, mass planting, flower arrangements |
| **Growth habit** | Clumping |

## Miscanthus sinensis 'Sacchariflorus'
(silver banner grass)

| | |
|---|---|
| **Pronunciation** | mis-KAN-thus sak-kar-ih-FLOR-us |
| **Zone** | 4–9 |
| **Form** | Tall, upright arching |
| **Size** | **Foliage** 5' (1.5 m) **Flower** 6' (2 m) **Width** 5' (1.5 m) |
| **Finest seasonal colour** | **Winter** blonde |
| **Flower colour & timing** | White, September |
| **Growing conditions** | Sun; ordinary garden conditions |
| **Landscape use** | Single, mass planting, flower arrangements |
| **Growth habit** | Invasive |

# grasses at a glance

## Miscanthus sinensis 'Sarabande'
(Japanese silver grass)

| | |
|---|---|
| **Pronunciation** | mis-KAN-thus sin-EN-sis |
| **Zone** | 4–9 |
| **Form** | Tall, upright arching |
| **Size** | Foliage 4' (1.2 m) Flower 5' (1.5 m) Width 3' (90 cm) |
| **Finest seasonal colour** | Autumn blonde |
| **Flower colour & timing** | White, September |
| **Growing conditions** | Sun; ordinary garden conditions |
| **Landscape use** | Single, mosaic, mass planting, flower arrangements |
| **Growth habit** | Clumping |

## Miscanthus sinensis 'Silberfeder'
(silver feather maiden grass)

| | |
|---|---|
| **Pronunciation** | mis-KAN-thus sin-EN-sis |
| **Zone** | 4–9 |
| **Form** | Tall, upright arching |
| **Size** | Foliage 6' (1.8 m) Flower 7' (2.1 m) Width 5' (1.5 m) |
| **Finest seasonal colour** | Winter blonde |
| **Flower colour & timing** | White, September |
| **Growing conditions** | Sun; ordinary garden conditions |
| **Landscape use** | Single, mass planting, flower arrangements |
| **Growth habit** | Clumping |

## Miscanthus sinensis 'Strictus'
(porcupine grass)

| | |
|---|---|
| **Pronunciation** | mis-KAN-thus sin-EN-sis STRIK-tus |
| **Zone** | 4–9 |
| **Form** | Tall, upright arching |
| **Size** | **Foliage** 5' (1.5 m) **Flower** 6' (1.8 m) **Width** 4' (1.2 m) |
| **Finest seasonal colour** | **Spring to summer** yellow variegated |
| **Flower colour & timing** | Bronze, October |
| **Growing conditions** | Sun; ordinary garden conditions to moist |
| **Landscape use** | Single, mass planting, flower arrangements |
| **Growth habit** | Clumping |

## Miscanthus sinensis 'Variegatus'
(variegated Japanese silver grass)

| | |
|---|---|
| **Pronunciation** | mis-KAN-thus sin-EN-sis var-ee-uh-GAH-tus |
| **Zone** | 4–9 |
| **Form** | Tall, upright arching |
| **Size** | **Foliage** 5' (1.5 m) **Flower** 6' (1.8 m) **Width** 5' (1.5 m) |
| **Finest seasonal colour** | **Summer and autumn** white variegated |
| **Flower colour & timing** | Bronze, November |
| **Growing conditions** | Sun; ordinary garden conditions |
| **Landscape use** | Single, mass planting, flower arrangements |
| **Growth habit** | Clumping |

# grasses at a glance

## Miscanthus sinensis 'Yaku Jima'
(Yaku Jima Japanese silver grass)

| | |
|---|---|
| **Pronunciation** | mis-KAN-thus sin-EN-sis YAH-koo JEE-mah |
| **Zone** | 4–9 |
| **Form** | Tall, upright arching |
| **Size** | Foliage 4' (1.2 m) Flower 5' (1.5 m) Width 3' (90 cm) |
| **Finest seasonal colour** | Autumn blonde, leaves are fine textured |
| **Flower colour & timing** | Pinkish, October |
| **Growing conditions** | Sun; ordinary garden conditions |
| **Landscape use** | Single, mosaic, mass planting, flower arrangements |
| **Growth habit** | Clumping |

## Miscanthus sinensis 'Zebrinus'
(zebra grass)

| | |
|---|---|
| **Pronunciation** | mis-KAN-thus sin-EN-sis zeh-BREYE-nus |
| **Zone** | 4–9 |
| **Form** | Tall, upright arching |
| **Size** | Foliage 5' (1.5 m) Flower 6' (1.8 m) Width 5' (1.5 m) |
| **Finest seasonal colour** | Spring to summer yellow variegated |
| **Flower colour & timing** | Pinkish, late September–early October |
| **Growing conditions** | Sun; ordinary garden conditions |
| **Landscape use** | Single, mass planting; flower arrangements, screen |
| **Growth habit** | Clumping |

## Molinia caerulea ssp. **arundinacea 'Skyracer'**
(tall purple moor grass)

| | |
|---|---|
| **Pronunciation** | moh-LIN-ee-ah se-RU-le-a |
| **Zone** | 4–8 |
| **Form** | Tall upright divergent |
| **Size** | **Foliage** 3' (90 cm) **Flower** 8' (2.4 m) **Width** 6' (1.8 m) |
| **Finest seasonal colour** | **Autumn** blonde |
| **Flower colour & timing** | Purplish turning light bronze, July–August |
| **Growing conditions** | Sun; ordinary garden conditions to moist |
| **Landscape use** | Single, mass planting |
| **Growth habit** | Clumping |

## Molinia caerulea 'Heidebraut'
(moor grass)

| | |
|---|---|
| **Pronunciation** | moh-LIN-ee-ah ser-OO-lee-ah |
| **Zone** | 4–8 |
| **Form** | Medium, upright divergent |
| **Size** | **Foliage** 1' (60 cm) **Flower** 3' (90 cm) **Width** 2' (60 cm) |
| **Finest seasonal colour** | **Autumn** blonde |
| **Flower colour & timing** | Purplish turning light bronze, July–August |
| **Growing conditions** | Sun to shade; ordinary garden conditions |
| **Landscape use** | Single, containers, mass planting |
| **Growth habit** | Clumping |

# grasses at a glance

**Molinia caerulea 'Moorhexe'**
(purple moor grass)

| | |
|---|---|
| **Pronunciation** | moh-LIN-ee-ah ser-OO-lee-ah |
| **Zone** | 4–8 |
| **Form** | Medium, upright divergent |
| **Size** | **Foliage** 1' (30 cm) **Flower** 3' (90 cm) **Width** 2' (60 cm) |
| **Finest seasonal colour** | **Autumn** blonde |
| **Flower colour & timing** | Purplish turning light bronze, July–August |
| **Growing conditions** | Sun to shade; ordinary garden conditions |
| **Landscape use** | Single, containers, mass planting |
| **Growth habit** | Clumping |

**Molinia caerulea 'Variegata'**
(variegated moor grass)

| | |
|---|---|
| **Pronunciation** | moh-LIN-ee-ah ser-OO-lee-ah ver-ee-uh-GAH-tah |
| **Zone** | 4–8 |
| **Form** | Medium, arching |
| **Size** | **Foliage** 18" (45 cm) **Flower** 30" (75 cm) **Width** 2' (60 cm) |
| **Finest seasonal colour** | **Spring to summer** yellow variegated |
| **Flower colour & timing** | Golden, July–August |
| **Growing conditions** | Sun to shade; ordinary garden conditions |
| **Landscape use** | Single, containers, mass planting |
| **Growth habit** | Clumping |

**Panicum virgatum**
(switch grass)

| | |
|---|---|
| **Pronunciation** | PAN-ih-kum veer-GAH-tum |
| **Zone** | 4–9 |
| **Form** | Medium, arching |
| **Size** | **Foliage** 3' (90 cm) **Flower** 4' (1.2 m) **Width** 4' (1.2 m) |
| **Finest seasonal colour** | **Autumn** yellow |
| **Flower colour & timing** | Pinkish turning brown, July–August |
| **Growing conditions** | Sun; ordinary garden conditions to moist |
| **Landscape use** | Single, mass planting, naturalizing |
| **Growth habit** | Clumping |

**Panicum virgatum 'Heavy Metal'**
(blue switch grass)

| | |
|---|---|
| **Pronunciation** | PAN-ih-kum veer-GAH-tum |
| **Zone** | 4–9 |
| **Form** | Tall, upright erect |
| **Size** | **Foliage** 3' (90 cm) **Flower** 4' (1.2 m) **Width** 3' (90 cm) |
| **Finest seasonal colour** | **Spring to summer** blue **Autumn and winter** red/blonde |
| **Flower colour & timing** | Pinkish turning brown, July–August |
| **Growing conditions** | Sun; ordinary garden conditions |
| **Landscape use** | Single, mass planting |
| **Growth habit** | Clumping |

# grasses at a glance

**Panicum virgatum 'Huron Solstice'**
(Huron switch grass)

| | |
|---|---|
| **Pronunciation** | PAN-ih-kum veer-GAH-tum |
| **Zone** | 4–9 |
| **Form** | Medium, upright erect |
| **Size** | Foliage 3' (90 cm) Flower 4' (1.2 m) Width 3' (90 cm) |
| **Finest seasonal colour** | Spring to summer burgundy Autumn and winter red/blonde |
| **Flower colour & timing** | Pinkish turning brown, July–August |
| **Growing conditions** | Sun; ordinary garden conditions |
| **Landscape use** | Single, mass planting |
| **Growth habit** | Clumping |

**Panicum virgatum 'Prairie Sky'**
(blue switch grass)

| | |
|---|---|
| **Pronunciation** | PAN-ih-kum veer-GAH-tum |
| **Zone** | 4–9 |
| **Form** | Medium, upright erect |
| **Size** | Foliage 3' (90 cm) Flower 4' (1.2 m) Width 3' (90 cm) |
| **Finest seasonal colour** | Spring to summer blue Autumn and winter red/blonde |
| **Flower colour & timing** | Pinkish turning brown, July–August |
| **Growing conditions** | Sun; ordinary garden conditions |
| **Landscape use** | Single, mass planting |
| **Growth habit** | Clumping |

## Panicum virgatum 'Rehbraun'
(switch grass)

| | |
|---|---|
| **Pronunciation** | PAN-ih-kum veer-GAH-tum |
| **Zone** | 4–9 |
| **Form** | Medium, arching |
| **Size** | **Foliage** 3' (90 cm) **Flower** 4' (1.2 m) **Width** 4' (1.2 m) |
| **Finest seasonal colour** | **Autumn to winter** red |
| **Flower colour & timing** | Pinkish turning brown, July–August |
| **Growing conditions** | Sun; ordinary garden conditions |
| **Landscape use** | Single, mass planting |
| **Growth habit** | Clumping |

## Panicum virgatum 'Shenandoah'
(switch grass)

| | |
|---|---|
| **Pronunciation** | PAN-ih-kum veer-GAH-tum |
| **Zone** | 4–9 |
| **Form** | Medium, arching |
| **Size** | **Foliage** 3' (90 cm) **Flower** 4' (1.2 m) **Width** 4' (1.2 m) |
| **Finest seasonal colour** | **Summer to autumn** red |
| **Flower colour & timing** | Purplish turning brown, July–August |
| **Growing conditions** | Sun; ordinary garden conditions |
| **Landscape use** | Single, mass planting |
| **Growth habit** | Clumping |

# grasses at a glance

**Panicum virgatum 'Warrior'**
(switch grass)

| | |
|---|---|
| **Pronunciation** | PAN-ih-kum veer-GAH-tum |
| **Zone** | 4–9 |
| **Form** | Medium, arching |
| **Size** | **Foliage** 3' (90 cm) **Flower** 4' (1.2 m) **Width** 4' (1.2 m) |
| **Finest seasonal colour** | **Autumn to winter** red |
| **Flower colour & timing** | Purplish turning brown, July–August |
| **Growing conditions** | Sun; ordinary garden conditions |
| **Landscape use** | Single, mass planting |
| **Growth habit** | Clumping |

**Pennisetum alopecuroides**
(hardy fountain grass)

| | |
|---|---|
| **Pronunciation** | pen-ih-SEE-tum al-oh-pek-yur-OY-deez |
| **Zone** | 5–9 |
| **Form** | Medium, arching |
| **Size** | **Foliage** 30" (75 cm) **Flower** 3' (90 cm) **Width** 3' (90 cm) |
| **Finest seasonal colour** | **Autumn and winter** yellow |
| **Flower colour & timing** | Pinkish, July–August |
| **Growing conditions** | Sun; ordinary garden conditions |
| **Landscape use** | Single, mass planting, flower arrangements |
| **Growth habit** | Clumping |

## Pennisetum alopecuroides 'Hameln'
(miniature fountain grass)

| | |
|---|---|
| **Pronunciation** | pen-ih-SEE-tum al-oh-pek-yur-OY-deez HAH-muln |
| **Zone** | 5–9 |
| **Form** | Small, arching |
| **Size** | **Foliage** 18" (36 cm) **Flower** 2' (60 cm) **Width** 2' (60 cm) |
| **Finest seasonal colour** | **Autumn to winter** yellow |
| **Flower colour & timing** | Whitish, July–August |
| **Growing conditions** | Sun; ordinary garden conditions |
| **Landscape use** | Single, groundcover, mass planting |
| **Growth habit** | Clumping |

## Pennisetum alopecuroides 'Little Bunny'
(fountain grass)

| | |
|---|---|
| **Pronunciation** | pen-ih-SEE-tum al-oh-pek-yur-OY-deez |
| **Zone** | 5–9 |
| **Form** | Small, tufted |
| **Size** | **Foliage** 8" (20 cm) **Flower** 1' (30 cm) **Width** 18" (45 cm) |
| **Finest seasonal colour** | **Spring to summer** green leaves |
| **Flower colour & timing** | Whitish, July–August |
| **Growing conditions** | Sun; ordinary garden conditions |
| **Landscape use** | Single, mass planting |
| **Growth habit** | Clumping |

# grasses at a glance

**Pennisetum alopecuroides 'Little Honey'**
(fountain grass)

| | |
|---|---|
| **Pronunciation** | pen-ih-SEE-tum al-oh-pek-yur-OY-deez |
| **Zone** | 5–9 |
| **Form** | Small, tufted |
| **Size** | Foliage 8" (20 cm) Flower 1' (30 cm) Width 18" (45 cm) |
| **Finest seasonal colour** | Spring to summer white variegated |
| **Flower colour & timing** | Whitish, July–August |
| **Growing conditions** | Sun; ordinary garden conditions |
| **Landscape use** | Single, mass planting |
| **Growth habit** | Clumping |

**Pennisetum alopecuroides 'Moudry'**
(black-flowering fountain grass)

| | |
|---|---|
| **Pronunciation** | pen-ih-SEE-tum al-oh-pek-yur-OY-deez MOU-dree |
| **Zone** | 5–9 |
| **Form** | Medium, arching |
| **Size** | Foliage 3' (90 cm) Flower 4' (1.2 m) Width 3' (90 cm) |
| **Finest seasonal colour** | Spring to summer green |
| **Flower colour & timing** | Purplish black, September |
| **Growing conditions** | Sun to semi-shade; ordinary garden conditions |
| **Landscape use** | Single, mass planting |
| **Growth habit** | Clumping |

## Pennisetum glaucum
(red-leafed millet)

| | |
|---|---|
| **Pronunciation** | pen-ih-SEE-tum GLOU-kum |
| **Zone** | 8–10 |
| **Form** | Annual, tall, arching |
| **Size** | Foliage 4' (1.2 m) Flower 5' (1.5 m) Width 2' (60 cm) |
| **Finest seasonal colour** | Spring to summer burgundy |
| **Flower colour & timing** | Burgundy, July |
| **Growing conditions** | Sun; ordinary garden conditions |
| **Landscape use** | Single, mosaic, mass plantings, flower arrangements |
| **Growth habit** | Clumping |

## Pennisetum messiacum 'Red Bunny Tails'
(Red Bunny Tails fountain grass)

| | |
|---|---|
| **Pronunciation** | pen-ih-SEE-tum |
| **Zone** | 8–10 |
| **Form** | Annual, medium, arching |
| **Size** | Foliage 2' (60 cm) Flower 3' (90 cm) Width 3' (90 cm) |
| **Finest seasonal colour** | Spring to summer burgundy tones |
| **Flower colour & timing** | Blonde with a tint of red, July |
| **Growing conditions** | Sun; ordinary garden conditions |
| **Landscape use** | Single, mosaic, mass plantings, flower arrangements |
| **Growth habit** | Clumping |

# grasses at a glance

**Pennisetum orientale**
(Oriental fountain grass)

| | |
|---|---|
| **Pronunciation** | pen-ih-SEE-tum or-ee-en-TAL-ee |
| **Zone** | 6–9 |
| **Form** | Small, arching |
| **Size** | Foliage 18" (36 cm) Flower 2' (60 cm) Width 2' (60 cm) |
| **Finest seasonal colour** | Summer to autumn early pink flowers |
| **Flower colour & timing** | Whitish, July–August |
| **Growing conditions** | Sun; ordinary garden conditions |
| **Landscape use** | Single, groundcover, mass planting |
| **Growth habit** | Clumping |

**Pennisetum setaceum 'Burgundy Giant'**
(giant purple-leaved fountain grass)

| | |
|---|---|
| **Pronunciation** | pen-ih-SEE-tum seh-TAY-see-um |
| **Zone** | 8–10 |
| **Form** | Annual, tall, arching |
| **Size** | Foliage 4' (1.2 m) Flower 5' (1.5 m) Width 3' (90 cm) |
| **Finest seasonal colour** | Spring to summer burgundy |
| **Flower colour & timing** | Burgundy, July–August |
| **Growing conditions** | Sun; ordinary garden conditions |
| **Landscape use** | Single, mosaic, mass plantings, flower arrangements |
| **Growth habit** | Clumping |

grasses at a glance  183

**Pennisetum setaceum 'Eaton Canyon'**
(dwarf purple-leaved fountain grass)

| | |
|---|---|
| **Pronunciation** | pen-ih-SEE-tum seh-TAY-see-um |
| **Zone** | 8–10 |
| **Form** | Annual, medium, arching |
| **Size** | **Foliage** 1' (30 cm) **Flower** 2' (60 cm) **Width** 2' (60 cm) |
| **Finest seasonal colour** | **Spring to summer** burgundy |
| **Flower colour & timing** | Burgundy, July–August |
| **Growing conditions** | Sun; ordinary garden conditions |
| **Landscape use** | Single, mosaic, mass plantings, flower arrangements |
| **Growth habit** | Clumping |

**Pennisetum setaceum 'Rubrum'**
(purple-leaved fountain grass)

| | |
|---|---|
| **Pronunciation** | pen-ih-SEE-tum seh-TAY-see-um ROO-brum |
| **Zone** | 8–10 |
| **Form** | Annual, medium, arching |
| **Size** | **Foliage** 2' (60 cm) **Flower** 3' (90 cm) **Width** 3' (90 cm) |
| **Finest seasonal colour** | **Spring to summer** burgundy |
| **Flower colour & timing** | Burgundy, July–August |
| **Growing conditions** | Sun; ordinary garden conditions |
| **Landscape use** | Single, mosaic, mass planting, flower arrangements |
| **Growth habit** | Clumping |

# grasses at a glance

**Pennisetum setaceum 'Ruppelii'**
(annual fountain grass)

| | |
|---|---|
| **Pronunciation** | pen-ih-SEE-tum  seh-TAY-see-um |
| **Zone** | 8–10 |
| **Form** | Annual, medium, arching |
| **Size** | **Foliage** 2' (60 cm) **Flower** 3' (90 cm) **Width** 3' (90 cm) |
| **Finest seasonal colour** | **Spring to summer** Burgundy |
| **Flower colour & timing** | Burgundy pink, July |
| **Growing conditions** | Sun; ordinary garden conditions |
| **Landscape use** | Single, mosaic, mass plantings, flower arrangements |
| **Growth habit** | Clumping |

**Phalaris arundinacea 'Picta'**
(ribbon grass)

| | |
|---|---|
| **Pronunciation** | fah-LAR-is ah-run-din-AH-see-ah |
| **Zone** | 4–9 |
| **Form** | Medium, upright arching |
| **Size** | **Foliage** 2' (60 cm) **Flower** 3' (90 cm) **Width** 3' (90 cm) |
| **Finest seasonal colour** | **Summer** white variegated |
| **Flower colour & timing** | White, June–July |
| **Growing conditions** | Sun to shade; ordinary garden conditions to moist |
| **Landscape use** | Single, containers, mass planting |
| **Growth habit** | Invasive |

## Phalaris arundinacea 'Feesey's Form'
(strawberries and cream ribbon grass)

| | |
|---|---|
| **Pronunciation** | fah-LAR-is ah-run-din-AH-see-ah |
| **Zone** | 4–9 |
| **Form** | Medium, upright arching |
| **Size** | Foliage 2' (60 cm) Flower 3' (90 cm) Width 3' (90 cm) |
| **Finest seasonal colour** | Summer to autumn white variegated |
| **Flower colour & timing** | White, June–July |
| **Growing conditions** | Sun to shade; ordinary garden conditions to moist |
| **Landscape use** | Single, containers, mass planting |
| **Growth habit** | Invasive |

## Saccharum ravennae (prev. Erianthus ravennae)
(hardy pampas grass)

| | |
|---|---|
| **Pronunciation** | sa-KAR-um ra-VEN-nay |
| **Zone** | 5–9 |
| **Form** | Tall, upright arching |
| **Size** | Foliage 5' (1.5 m) Flower 15' (4.6 m) Width 5' (1.5m) |
| **Finest seasonal colour** | Spring to summer green Autumn blonde |
| **Flower colour & timing** | Silvery-purple, August |
| **Growing conditions** | Sun; ordinary garden conditions |
| **Landscape use** | Single, mosaic, mass planting |
| **Growth habit** | Clumping |

# grasses at a glance

**Schizachyrium scoparium**
(little bluestem)

| | |
|---|---|
| **Pronunciation** | skits-ah-KEER-ee-um skoh-PAIR-ee-um |
| **Zone** | 4–9 |
| **Form** | Medium, upright divergent |
| **Size** | **Foliage** 2' (60 cm) **Flower** 3' (90 cm) **Width** 2' (60 cm) |
| **Finest seasonal colour** | **Autumn to winter** red/bronze |
| **Flower colour & timing** | Bronze, August–September |
| **Growing conditions** | Sun; ordinary garden conditions to dry |
| **Landscape use** | Single, naturalizing, mass planting, flower arrangements |
| **Growth habit** | Clumping |

**Sesleria autumnalis**
(autumn moor grass)

| | |
|---|---|
| **Pronunciation** | sez-LAIR-ee-ah aw-TUM-nal-is |
| **Zone** | 5–9 |
| **Form** | Medium, arching |
| **Size** | **Foliage** 1' (30 cm) **Flower** 2' (60 cm) **Width** 2' (60 cm) |
| **Finest seasonal colour** | **Autumn** bright yellow |
| **Flower colour & timing** | Purplish-black, September |
| **Growing conditions** | Sun; ordinary garden conditions |
| **Landscape use** | Single, mass planting, naturalizing, groundcover |
| **Growth habit** | Clumping |

## Sorghastrum nutans 'Sioux Blue'
(Indian grass)

| | |
|---|---|
| **Pronunciation** | sor-GAS-trum NOO-tanz |
| **Zone** | 4–9 |
| **Form** | Medium, upright arching |
| **Size** | **Foliage** 3' (90 cm) **Flower** 5' (1.5 cm) **Width** 3' (90 cm) |
| **Finest seasonal colour** | **Summer** blue **Autumn** golden yellow |
| **Flower colour & timing** | Golden-bronze, August–September |
| **Growing conditions** | Sun; ordinary garden conditions to dry |
| **Landscape use** | Single, naturalizing; flower arrangements |
| **Growth habit** | Clumping |

## Spartina pectinata 'Aureomarginata'
(prairie cord grass)

| | |
|---|---|
| **Pronunciation** | spar-TEE-nah pek-tin-AH-tah |
| **Zone** | 4–7 |
| **Form** | Tall, upright arching |
| **Size** | **Foliage** 3' (90 cm) **Flower** 5' (1.5 m) **Width** 3' (90 cm) |
| **Finest seasonal colour** | **Summer** yellow variegated |
| **Flower colour & timing** | Golden, August–September |
| **Growing conditions** | Sun; ordinary garden conditions |
| **Landscape use** | Single, mass planting, naturalizing |
| **Growth habit** | Moderately invasive |

# grasses at a glance

**Sporobolus heterolepis**
(prairie dropseed)

| | |
|---|---|
| **Pronunciation** | spor-AH-bol-us het-er-oh-LEP-is |
| **Zone** | 4–8 |
| **Form** | Medium, arching |
| **Size** | **Foliage** 1' (30 cm) **Flower** 2' (60 cm) **Width** 2' (60 cm) |
| **Finest seasonal colour** | **Autumn** bronze |
| **Flower colour & timing** | Scented bronze, August |
| **Growing conditions** | Sun; ordinary garden conditions |
| **Landscape use** | Single, mass planting, naturalizing |
| **Growth habit** | Clumping |

**Stipa tenuissima**
(Mexican feather grass)

| | |
|---|---|
| **Pronunciation** | STYE-pah ten-yoo-ISS-ih-mah |
| **Zone** | 6–10 |
| **Form** | Medium, arching |
| **Size** | **Foliage** 1' (30 cm) **Flower** 2' (60 cm) **Width** 1' (30 cm) |
| **Finest seasonal colour** | **Summer** light green |
| **Flower colour & timing** | White, July |
| **Growing conditions** | Sun; ordinary garden conditions |
| **Landscape use** | Single, mass planting, naturalizing |
| **Growth habit** | Clumping |

# selected reading

Baker, Mary E. F. *The Book of Grasses.* Garden City: Doubleday, 1912.

Brooklyn Botanic Garden Record. *Plants & Gardens: Ornamental Grasses.* Brooklyn: Brooklyn Botanic Garden, Inc., 1988.

Brookes, John. *The Book of Garden Design.* New York: Macmillan, 1991

Darke, Rick. *For Your Garden: Ornamental Grasses.* Toronto: Little, Brown & Co., 1994.

Darke, Rick. *The Colour Encyclopedia of Ornamental Grasses.* Portland, OR: Timber Press, 1999.

Greenlee, John. *The Encyclopedia of Ornamental Grasses.* New York: Michael Friedman Publishing Group, Inc., 1992.

Hawley, Patricia. *Grasses.* Aylesbury, Bucks, UK: Shire Publications, 1989.

Jekyll, Gertrude. *Colour Schemes for the Garden.* (Reprint) Antique Collectors' Club, 1982.

Johnson, Lorraine. *The Ontario Naturalized Garden: The Complete Guide to Using Native Plants.* North Vancouver: Whitecap Books, 1995.

King, Michael and Piet Oudolf. *Gardening with Grasses.* Portland, OR: Timber Press, 1998.

Macself, Albert James. *Grass.* London: Cecil Palmer, 1924.

Madson, John. *Where The Sky Began: Land Of The Tallgrass Prairie.* Boston: Houghton Mifflin Company, 1982.

Oakes, A.J. *Ornamental Grasses and Grasslike Plants.* Scarborough, ON: Nelson Canada, 1990.

Oudolf, Piet with Noël Kingsbury. *Designing with Plants.* Portland, OR: Timber Press, 1999.

Reinhardt, Thomas, Marina Reinhardt, and Mark Moscowitz. *Ornamental Grass Gardening: Design Idea, Functions and Effects.* New York: Michael Friedman Publishing Group, 1994.

Taylor, Nigel J. *Ornamental Grasses, Bamboos, Rushes & Sedges.* New York: Sterling Publishing Co., 1992.

# index
*Grasses listed appear in illustrations or photographs

**Edited** Elaine Jones
**Proofread** Lesley Cameron
**Cover design** Roberta Batchelor
**Interior design** Stacey Noyes / LuzForm Design
**Photographs** Martin Quinn
**Illustrations** Wendy Hogenbirk

**Printed and bound in Canada by Friesens**


**National Library of Canada Cataloguing in Publication Data**
Quinn, Martin, 1949-
  Grass scapes : gardening with ornamental grasses / Martin Quinn, Catherine Macleod.

  Includes index.
  ISBN 1-55285-343-8

  1. Ornamental grasses. I. Title.
SB431.7.Q56 2003      635.9'349      C2003910255-6

The publisher acknowledges the support of the Canada Council for the Arts and the Cultural Services Branch of the Government of British Columbia for our publishing program. We acknowledge the financial support of the Government of Canada through the Book Publishing Industry Development Program for our publishing activities.